on the
FRONT LINES

on the
FRONT LINES

Bahá'í Youth in Their Own Words

edited by
Aaron Emmel & Heather Brandon

George Ronald • Oxford

George Ronald, *Publisher*
46 High Street, Kidlington, Oxford OX5 2DN

*A catalogue record for this book is available
from the British Library*

ISBN 0-85398-464-6

Typesetting & Cover Design by Alexander Leith
www.yander.com

Printed in Great Britain by Biddles Ltd.
www.biddles.co.uk

Contents

CONTENTS

Introduction

Heather Brandon

O*ne* magazine began in early 1996. I remember the very meeting I register as its origin. My new husband, River, and I had just moved to an apartment in an old, spacious red schoolhouse in Kittery, Maine, from a small, dark abode in Plymouth, New Hampshire. We had been the only Bahá'ís in Plymouth, and although there weren't many in Kittery, our new home was near Green Acre Bahá'í School and the relatively bustling Eliot community and its environs. Many young Bahá'ís lived in the area at the time but most of them were a good five years our junior and unmarried. We decided to invite as many as would come to our apartment for a get-to-know-you session. Many of the Bahá'í youth in the area did not seem to know each other's names and didn't associate with one another. Some of them were members of the Bahá'í high school band, Agents of Change, and others who were not in this band made a clear point of it. Being new to the scene, I thought I could help to bridge the gap or find a new project for some of us to work on.

There were about 19 of us at the meeting, which took place on the first day of the Bahá'í fast that year. Ages ranged from 11 or 12 to River and me, the oldest at 24. We did some ice-breaker activities sitting around in a big circle. The younger ones had their eyes directed downward and the louder, more confident ones were cracking uncomfortable jokes and pushing each other playfully. I wanted to share my idea of working on a local newsletter together but it was hard to find the right moment. I couldn't force people to my will.

Finally the group settled down and the subject arose of working on something together, having regular meetings with a purpose. There were models for such things, like the Bahá'í Youth Workshops that had sprung up across the US. I saw my window of opportunity and took it. Others were interested. Yes, a newsletter could be a great project. We could put movie listings in it and band reviews and talk about some Bahá'í topics. It could be for the Bahá'í youth in the local area – maybe even people in Boston would be interested in it.

Immediately the conversation turned to what the newsletter could be called. We had a massive brainstorming session. People threw out as many names as they could think of and a scribe wrote them all down. Once we couldn't think of any more wild and crazy names, we started narrowing them down. The group more or less agreed on which names were awful and we crossed those out. If one or two people still thought *Mucous* was an awesome name, everyone convinced them that it wouldn't work. In the end, we were left with *The Force* and *One*. We took a vote to make the decision. (To this day, I'm sure there are people from that meeting who will one day start a magazine called *The Force*.)

So there it began. At later meetings, as we worked on what would be included in the newsletter, we also designed a logo, consulted about the newsletter's format and brainstormed ways to fund its production. We agreed that once every two Bahá'í months was probably a good release schedule, giving us enough time to pull together material, edit, design and produce it. Before a month had passed, we realized we had no small newsletter; we had a 'zine.

Surrounding Local Spiritual Assemblies agreed to help fund our initial efforts and we committed ourselves to finding subscribers. We assigned people to various editorial, sales and production roles. I became co-managing editor with Amelia Davis, who at that time was about 17, lived down the road from me and was not a Bahá'í (she is now). River became head of production and design and our home graphic design office was transformed into *One* magazine headquarters.

Kalím Armstrong, 17 and from Durham, New Hampshire, headed up local sales. We made 15 or 20 cardboard display boxes that could both showcase magazines and hold a small supply of quarters and dollar bills in a slotted box. These boxes were spray-painted black and emblazoned with the *One* logo. We took them to various cafes, music and book shops and convenience stores in the area. The money from these sales was harvested weekly or so and only a couple of the boxes were stolen or demolished. Some stores wouldn't take them because of the religious affiliation. We made no secret that ours was a Bahá'í effort. Gradually, Bahá'ís in the area subscribed and by the time our third issue came out we knew we weren't charging enough for our magazine. Slowly we learned how to run a business from the ground up. Our methods improved and our group consultative process received a lot of time and attention as we struggled to offer our all to the magazine.

My own goal with *One* was a little subversive. I wanted the Bahá'ís to awaken to how amazing, deep, cool, wonderful and excellent it is to be a Bahá'í. I wanted to reach Bahá'í youth, their parents, their friends, right where they lived. This meant that the design had to be infused with a certain what-the-heck-is-this energy that made people really look. As we developed the look and feel, I made my opinion known rather than distancing myself just because I was the editor. I think everyone had this attitude: the whole magazine belonged to all of us, so why remain silent on an issue? And we all wanted the magazine to stand out and compete with other hot magazines for young people at the time, yet rise above them with its spiritual righteousness. We entered a 'cooler-than-thou' competition of sorts, although it wasn't clear, exactly, who we were competing with. We wanted people to see the Bahá'í Faith as a very cool thing to join if they weren't already a part of it. We discovered our own unique expression through words and images. We didn't have to feel religious and stuffy.

The writing had to be good. The grammar had to be perfect but not ostentatiously so. The language had to be clever, interesting, dragging you into itself. Article titles had to read well and look good. And so on. All of this had to happen in a sort of mysterious way, like feeling one's way through darkness for a light switch. Most of the time we did not hit it right on but when we did an issue well, or an article really stood out, we felt it. People around us just glowed with love for what they read and we got a lot of wonderful feedback about what we were doing.

Often when I brainstormed potential articles or writers, I was using my right brain, where you try not to think too hard about what you are doing. It just had to feel right. I knew the general thing I was going for and I only knew I was doing it right if I looked through a final piece and got goose bumps.

Our staff began to solidify after a while, still including people as young as 12. We trained some people how to use the computers, mostly Photoshop or QuarkXPress. Others were more proficient at writing or helping to find others to write articles. Santina Vu, from Sanford, Maine, and only 12 at the time, became a stellar subscription recorder and bookkeeper, with River's close guidance. Her older brother, Nguyen, 13 when he started working on the magazine, was a whiz at Photoshop and had endless enthusiasm for attending the magazine meetings.

The core group of people who started *One* filtered away after six months to a year as they graduated from high school and left for college in other states. A majority of them ended up in California, which was a great loss for *One* in some respects but it had the advantage of increasing our reach for sales and subscriptions. *One* made it to Bosch Bahá'í School and gradually to the Native American Bahá'í Institute, Louhelen Bahá'í School and Louis Gregory Bahá'í Institute as well.

For several months the only regular local staff were River, me, Nguyen and Santina, with occasional visits from other interested people and the original staff when they were home from college. In order to survive, and to accommodate the growing need to have a legitimate, high-quality magazine, I had to reach beyond local Bahá'ís to maintain an editorial staff. So I used the Internet and email.

I wanted to create a manageable network of people that could function without straining itself, including people who could talk to each other and work together as well as pull together an interview or an essay without much notice. The ability to improvise on the groundwork was vital. The groundwork itself was constantly being revised, too, because we learned what worked and what didn't.

For instance, it helped to open up lines of communication completely and encouraged everyone to talk to everyone else. It didn't help to have lots of people look at an article and group-edit all the way through the process. Instead we needed to narrow down the number of people who looked at something and give one person the final say at any given stage of editing. The spirit remained the same through our revisions, though. Primarily we wanted a collaborative process to guide us.

INTRODUCTION

In a way, it was all about the image of what it means to be a Bahá'í. Because we're only talking about printed material here, not real life and deeds and work and communities and families. The image was all the magazine had and then the ideas it threw at you if you liked the image enough to let the ideas sink in, if you made yourself open to them. This was true regardless of the reader's religion or beliefs. My desire was to get readers excited enough to teach and share or at least feel good about Bahá'u'lláh.

What freed *One* completely was the lack of any agenda. We did not have to be the voice for an institution, communicate news or do anything at all formally. Any sense of authority came from the group of people who made it and we tried carefully to avoid sounding authoritative. Instead, the focus was on speaking what we saw as truth and reality, especially revealing things that we thought others would point to and agree with and feel was being voiced in some unusual way that attracted them. I think at least our better material accomplished this. But we had the freedom to publish goofy stuff that didn't necessarily mean anything deep, as well as material that was incredibly profound, heart-wrenching or intellectual. I knew that laughter was the key to opening hearts, so the magazine needed to make people laugh. But we approached all of that very seriously.

By the time a year had passed, we had created nine issues of *One* and had lined up themes for the whole second volume of magazines. I was hard at work realizing goals for the development of a comprehensive long-distance editorial staff network. I had faced the fact that *One* was actually a social and economic development project and I worked on a survey to compile ideas about skills that staff members were picking up in the process of their work. Before long I had assembled a manual to help us in our third volume of editorial work, which included an organizational map of how the entire staff related to one another, a list of editorial staff members and how to reach them, descriptions of the various sections of the magazine and how they should be approached, handouts for people to give to prospective contributors, a press release in case it was needed, rotation schedules for assignments, lists of themes and deadlines and guidelines for writing and getting art and poetry contributions. This manual went out to all the editorial staff for reference. Unfortunately, we never finished our second year of production but we had a huge backlog of material that reached halfway into volume three.

I was blown away by the amount of material waiting to be committed to ink and paper and the degree of passion in the hearts of the Bahá'í youth who sent us contributions. The themes we generated for each issue seemed to be a never-ending list of good ideas. Similarly, the staff who worked on the magazine seemed to get so much good out of the process. Gradually, most of work was done by email, so we never met face-to-face, but we grew to know each other and to find creative ways to get our work done.

The survey I undertook during the summer of 1997 yielded a long list of skills that the staff had acquired. Broadly speaking, we learned skills in design, writing, publishing and production, editing, consultation and communication, human resource management and other organizational skills, marketing, people- and resource-networking and financial management. We ended up learning so much that I find it important to share here some details about the skills we acquired. Through this learning process, I received a deep understanding of a divine process at work in all of us.

In the area of design skills, our staff became familiar with and learned how to use a variety of computer software, including Photoshop, Illustrator and QuarkXPress. We discussed aesthetics in general, such as composition and color, and taught practical layout techniques. The trial-and-error process inherent in our experimental design-then-publish method was very instructive. We learned about typography and the arduous process of publishing others' art from a variety of raw sources. We did almost everything in the sketch-to-final-product approach, which taught the staff how you get to a published paper from a mere intangible idea. And finally, we all enhanced our own artistic ability simply by using it, thinking about it and discussing it.

We invested a colossal amount of energy into our work on the written word. We covered some of the more elementary skills, like keyboard, use of the dictionary and thesaurus, general handling of language and grammar, and increasing our vocabulary. We moved on to how to grab and keep a reader's interest, speak to a relevant topic, feature salient points and satisfy the reader. One of the trickiest skills we worked on was mentioning Bahá'u'lláh and ways of referring to the Bahá'í Faith, with an eye towards random people encountering the magazine who had never heard of the Faith, as well as dedicated Bahá'í subscribers who didn't want to learn about it all over again in each article they read. Other important skills we learned, which apply to almost everything in life, included the ability to think critically and examine the written word, especially one's own, editing multiple times to yield an improved piece. The process of having others read and critique our work was cleansing, humbling, heartening and spiritualizing.

Many skills in magazine production and publishing routines were developed over the two years. We learned to balance our budget with our product and scale our creative ideas up or down accordingly. As a professional designer, River taught the rest of us the steps of the production process and he learned some new techniques himself from dealing with different printers. We gradually improved the look and had a bigger budget. Our second volume had a full-color cover and was very slick indeed compared to our first efforts. We learned how to innovate to make the product look as good as it could. We also learned to plan and meet deadlines within the entire idea-to-finished-product process and how to appreciate that process in the end.

The business of editing written pieces was challenging and posed several new obstacles for those of us in an editorial role. We had to push ourselves to question the writer, catching bad grammar or faulty idea flows where we could, encouraging improvement with clear communication skills. Editing over email versus in person was in some ways tremendously difficult but in other ways made things a lot easier. I found that, in person, I was more bashful and retiring in making suggestions or corrections and to compensate I would end up coming across as too forceful and blunt. I knew what would sound better but I was wary of offending a budding Ernest Hemingway or Maya Angelou. Over email, transactions took on a different character: constructive, loving criticism became the main thing to communicate. We worked to tease out what is vital and good in writing and to spell that out for the writers, ever pushing them to diminish the irrelevant, to write in a stimulating manner and to think of how they would come across, especially when discussing the Bahá'í Faith. We worked particularly hard to help people use Bahá'í texts in pertinent references, rather than quoting from the texts willy-nilly as a way to avoid speaking in their own voices. My mantra was 'If you can say it yourself, do so and quote Bahá'u'lláh sparingly'. I surprised myself with how strongly I felt about that at times because it seemed contrary to what we have heard about teaching. I found that it was easier to read Bahá'í texts straight from the source instead of planted in articles ostensibly written by other people.

When it came to consultation, we often told ourselves that the process was more important than the product. When things became tense during a meeting and ideas clashed strongly, sometimes over seemingly very minor topics, this notion was helpful to keep in mind. It was very easy to become attached to what the end result might be. When we reflected on the group process, and the spiritual reality of working collaboratively, it was easier to let go of those attachments. Prayer, as a foundation and a protection, was invaluable, and we became acutely aware of the Bahá'í texts as a vital reference in our work when we had questions about how to proceed. We gained respect for one another's work and effort, becoming increasingly aware of the process of Bahá'í consultation in action and the impact of a loving attitude and carefully-chosen words. Many on the staff developed a determination not to let things slide by, undiscussed, which yielded such qualities as vigilance, patience, detachment, honesty and a view of pitfalls and trials as possibly beneficial to our process. All of us grew to have a greater capacity to focus and carry out responsibilities.

The evolution of our staff network taught me the importance of planning. We set collaborative goals and met them, gradually under-standing and adapting to the sequence of the different phases of our work. Our management hierarchy took shape and we tried to clarify it and apply Bahá'í principles as one would in a workplace. I strove to set guidelines, abide by them and foster unity around them. The management process, for me, was the most instructive and inspiring of anything I did for the magazine and it was thus also the most rewarding.

Encouraging receptivity and interest in *One* magazine enabled us to develop another set of skills. We learned how to make sales calls and in-person pitches, introducing and explaining ourselves and our product. We innovated a price structure for wholesale and retail sales and managed a database of information. Our efforts naturally led to the need to negotiate plans and prices with various bodies. We had to create promotional materials for ourselves and feed every part of the marketing and sales cycle. Overall we had to hone our message and develop a clear identity so it could be understood and digested, and of course, purchased. The sales side of our work was difficult to comprehend at first because a part of us wanted people to get our magazine for free. We had to set sales goals in order to make the magazine possible. This took a lot more clarity and responsibility than we would have guessed at the outset.

Today, River and I are still living in Eliot and raising our three children. I dream about what lies in wait for me out there, new magazines to publish or yet more books to write and edit. The skills I developed while working on *One* will stay with me, as well as the friendships and working relationships I forged with people whose faces I've never seen, including my co-editor for this very book. Some day I still hope we might meet and reminisce over our brief time spent making a fantastic magazine, shaping ideas about what it meant to be a Bahá'í youth at the end of the 20th century, on the cusp of so many great things to come.

Foreword

Aaron Emmel

For a reason which now escapes me, I decided that Belize needed a youth newsletter. The National Bahá'í Youth Committee was unconvinced but said that I could use its resources to such an end as long as they could be kept out of it. (I was secretary of the Committee and the other members were wise enough to avoid any correspondence duties.) Thus *The Flame* was born.

I am sorry to say that I was responsible for the name, and although the Youth Committee as a whole was even less impressed with that title then than I am now, nothing better was presented. I printed the copies on a mechanical relic in the top room of the Bahá'í National Center in 1991. *The Flame*, one front and back page of news and announcements, was sent to youth across the small Caribbean country. It was met with a resounding lack of interest.

Undaunted, I composed and printed a second issue. If this is possible, it was met with even less enthusiasm. Although a few phone calls could mobilize entire communities of youth to activities a day's journey from their homes, the newsletters just never caught on. After I resigned to go to college in the United States, the Youth Committee never attempted another one.

Eventually I returned to Belize to upset old friends and disturb my parents. The day before my departure, I got bored. (I can no longer remember what being bored feels like but I would love to have enough time to experience it again.) I grabbed some art, poetry and prose various friends had afflicted me with and went to Kinko's. There I assembled them into an amateurish reminder of a magazine. I had time to force it upon some friends just before I left the country.

When I returned, someone (it was probably Elin Griffith – she always enjoyed causing me trouble) reminded me about the ill-conceived 'magazine' and suggested we turn it into something real. Never the one to dismiss potential disasters, I gathered a board of directors and *Be* magazine was launched as a non-profit organization.

Rather than bore you with the entire *Be* magazine story, as I did in the first draft, I'll just present the highlights. We covered the first multi-racial South African elections from the perspective of a Bahá'í youth. A staff member was shot at while watching TV and the lamp beside her head shattered. We had stories about teaching in newly-accessible Eastern European countries. We heard about being a Bahá'í youth in a country where teaching is illegal. We were ambushed by people spraying fire extinguishers at us. Our New Zealand version had to omit some pieces because they were considered to be too overwhelming. The computer and disks our layouts were on were stolen the day before the images were to go to the printer. All in all, it was quite an exciting time. And I learned a lot from the experience: specifically, I really, really should not have hired that layout artist.

I finished college in Hawaii. That involved teaching the Faith, dancing, swimming and playing beach volleyball, although I also went to some parties, discussed the Faith on the radio and wrote for a local paper for variety. Some of the high school students on Oahu had wanted a workshop for a while, so we started one, thereby institutionalizing the process of teaching the Faith, dancing, swimming and playing beach volleyball for future generations to enjoy. One morning, on my way to an Oahu Bahá'í Youth Workshop meeting, I saw an issue of the *American Bahá'í* lying on a table in the hallway of the Bahá'í Center. I picked it up and started reading it. There was now, I saw, a youth page. And the page was talking about a new magazine for Bahá'í youth called *One*.

It looked professional. It sounded exciting. I wanted to be involved.

The managing editor's name was Heather Brandon and the features editor (the features section was called 'On the Front Lines') was her sister-in-law, Oceana Brandon. They encouraged me to submit an article, so I did, of which Oceana then encouraged me to rewrite every other sentence.

I found myself glad that *Be* had folded because these people were better at this than I had been in every way. They were better editors, with more correspondents, great artwork, flawless layout and they were kind and encouraging to their writers. They had proven themselves with over a year's worth of well-designed, on-time issues.

Then Oceana resigned so that she could focus on her education. *One* asked if I would take over as features editor. I accepted.

The system was ingenious. The magazine had various sections. In addition to 'On the Front Lines' there was a restaurant/hangout/book/music review section called 'On the Scene' and an arts section called 'Off the Wall'. Heather coordinated all of these sections and the columns. There was also a design team, headed by Heather's husband (and Oceana's brother) River, a circulation department and a sales department. A lot of the staff was in or around Maine, where the magazine was headquartered, but the majority of us were situated around the country and had never met each other.

Each editorial department had a team of correspondents. Their responsibilities rotated. For example, in the 'On the Front Lines' section, for any given editorial period, two correspondents would be responsible for writing or soliciting essays, two would be responsible for interviews and two would have a break. (This is a simplification but it's generally how it worked.)

Each issue had a particular theme. If you read the pieces collected here (and I hope you will, since you're willing to squander your time on the Foreword), you'll probably be able to pick out which themes many of them were written for. ('I really like football, which, as it happens, relates directly to the unity of religions . . .') River and Heather's design company, Unit.E, maintained an email list for the staff and whenever I started work on a new issue, I would write down my ideas for the theme and send them to the whole staff. Then the staff could discuss ideas via email.

After this brainstorming session, I would assign essays and interviews and work with the writers to develop their ideas. Once the pieces were finished, they were posted to a password-protected Web site called Redline. I would invite the other editors and different correspondents for each issue to go to Redline and review one of the pieces. The comments they made were available for the writer to see. Once this process was finished, I would look over the comments to determine whether or not there were ideas that the author and I had missed that should be incorporated into the final draft.

During all of this, the 'On the Front Lines' correspondents could email each other on an email list set up for that specific department. There was also an email list specifically for the editorial department and email lists for each of the other sections. All of this helped us to feel connected despite the distance.

In 1997 the Eshraghieh and Mahmoud Rabbani Charitable Trust invited *One* magazine to give a presentation at an art seminar at the Bahá'í Conference on Social and Economic Development for the Americas. I flew to Orlando to represent the magazine along with 'On the Front Lines' correspondent Hope Turpin. We were excited about this because the reason we'd put so much effort into youth publications is that we consider them integral to the process of social development.

Materially, I consider humanity to be fine. We have more than enough food and energy to suffice everyone on the planet. (By some estimates, there is currently enough food for seven billion people and we currently have six billion. Of course, there are conflicting estimates – that's what makes these types of discussions so interesting.) But socially and mentally there are huge problems. To cite just one example, we haven't figured out how to make sure that everyone has access to our material wealth. In some communities, food is thrown away; in others, children starve.

In terms of the number of people influenced, just after parents and schools (including teachers, peers and curriculum), the media is the most important force in helping people decide who they are. The media defines the world and its parameters. It explains what roles are possible. It tells you where *you* fit in. Change the media and you change how people interact. Change a magazine, if it's a magazine that's read, and you change people's minds. That's why I've given so much time to youth publications. If you can make some isolated youth feel like he or she is part of a larger movement, that she's not alone, that it's not just okay but commendable to challenge her entire society and try to change the world, you've inspired a revolution that no number of guns can match.

Eventually, *One* magazine stopped coming out. We were all doing it for free and the production staff was waylaid by other demands in their lives. I kept bringing in and editing essays and interviews for a long time before I admitted that new issues of the magazine didn't seem to be coming to my house any more. But the material I was working on was too good to abandon.

That's why this book was put together. It shows the sweep of *One*'s contents, including material from both published and unpublished issues.

One shows a generation in transition. The interviews and essays present a diverse group of people who grew up learning that they carry responsibility for the future, who champion alien ideals in a crumbling society, who truly believe that they are here to transform a world they sometimes don't even fit into. Their writing lets them share their thoughts with other youth going through the same things. *One* has preserved a snapshot of why they're doing what they're doing – their hopes and joys and uncertainties. In *One* magazine we tried to tell a generation's worth of stories. This is what our friends were doing, feeling and thinking at the turn of the millennium.

Publisher's Note

One magazine was published in America by youth for youth. Many of the articles, particularly the interviews, contain colloquialisms and interjections which are typical of the language of youth. We have left these wherever possible as they give a liveliness, freshness and energy to the dialogue and are a true reflection of the individual authors.

1

Reflections on Freedom

Carrie Smith

Each human being's ultimate aim in life is to be free. We were created to have choice, driven by the ability to reason.

What is 'freedom' in the context of the Bahá'í Faith?

In my personal experience of trying to grasp the Bahá'í concept of freedom, I realized that the simple pleasures in my life are not it. This is not the freedom Bahá'u'lláh foretold.

I began to analyze my wants and desires. I discovered that those things I thought would bring me happiness – like a fully-furnished apartment or a new car – were only temporal pleasures and even more so when they were sought after for selfish reasons. Of course, such awakenings ignited my need to find the truth.

I found that the essence of true freedom is to be aware of the needs of humankind and then to participate in the evolutionary process of an ever-advancing civilization.

With this realization, material cravings suddenly became insignificant to me. They were not leading me towards true freedom.

But how am I going to maintain this level of awareness?

Naturally, I must have a strong spiritual foundation in the Covenant, thereby having a strong commitment to exemplifying the fundamental verities and ordinances of the Faith. But what is the driving force behind it all?

When I read about the lives of the heroes and devoted members of our beloved Cause, there is one aspect of their lives that radiates brighter than anything else: service to the Cause, hence service to humankind. Their constant ardor stemmed from an ongoing awareness of the need to be of service to humanity.

However, to be of service to humanity, the devoted loved ones of God knew and understood that each and every aspect of their lives had to reflect the divine way of life. Without this reciprocating effect, as the writings clearly say, we are restricted to the contingencies of this 'nether world' and we are slaves to its animalistic tendencies:

> And among the teachings of Bahá'u'lláh is man's freedom, that through the ideal Power he should be free and emancipated from the captivity of the world of nature . . .[1]

I can see the lack of spiritual freedom that surrounds us manifested in gross materialism, in the insane extremes of wealth and poverty and in cruel bigotries among people. Because God loves us, He gives us the choice to walk the path of attachment to idle fancies or to walk the path of real freedom in service to the Cause of God.

2

Inside Out:
Justice and True Liberty

Amelia Villagómez

Bush-trimming time has come again in my family, the time of the year that makes me clench my teeth and wish I could turn transparent to camouflage myself in the air and wind. But there is no escaping this dreaded ritual at my house.

In our backyard, bushes, ten feet tall or more, border the fence. Usually by spring, neither our fence nor the roof of our neighbor's yard is visible, so we need to get those clippers out and chop away. Everyone in the family finds his or her assigned station and forms an assembly line. My father and brother trim the bushes and I gather the trimmings neatly into piles. Then my grandfather takes the piles to the side of the road where the garbage collector hauls them away to a dump. My mother, as usual, serves as the gopher but still finds time to direct our progress and urges us to work harder and faster.

Today, while I worked I thought of how Bahá'u'lláh created so many metaphors with trees, such as comparing us to the leaves of one tree. I decided to take a closer look at the trees in the yard and hopefully learn something from them. As I watched the cutting and moving of branches from yard to garbage, I noticed something.

I imagined God as the tree and us, His creation, as the branches that sprout from the tree. When the branch is connected to the tree, the branch receives nourishment from the roots. But what happens when the branch is cut off from its source? For a few days, the branch survives on its stored nutrients but soon the leaves on the branch wilt and the branch dies because of its separation from the tree. Without the tree, the branch is helpless. Only through the tree's bounty do the branches grow.

Like the branches, when we disobey God or the Covenant, we cut ourselves off from our source. When we cut ourselves off from God, we deny ourselves the mercies and bounties that He has to offer. God provides us with love, life, and purpose; and so, like the branches, without Him we are helpless. We cannot cut ourselves off from God and expect to remain healthy and happy. In the Hidden Words, Bahá'u'lláh reveals, 'Love Me, that I may love thee. If thou lovest Me not, My love can in no wise reach thee. Know this, O servant.'[2]

In the United States, health and happiness are often said to go hand in hand with being independent. Americans like to think that everyone is entitled to do and say whatever they want. Freedom is guaranteed to all and all use and accept it with open arms.

Bahá'u'lláh talks about liberty in a different way:

> True liberty consisteth in man's submission unto My commandments, little as ye know it . . . Say: The liberty that profiteth you is to be found nowhere except in complete servitude unto God, the Eternal Truth.[3]

Although we may not always understand why Bahá'u'lláh has given us certain laws, we must obey them so we can experience true liberty.

I once talked with some Bahá'ís about their experience of going to parties and not doing drugs and drinking with their peers. One Bahá'í told me that he explained to his friend, 'Life is so wonderful. Why would you want to take something that makes you less conscious and less able to savor it?' By listening to God, we can remain connected to the tree that fills us all with blessings and love, and by being blessed, don't we have more freedom in life, the kind of freedom that really matters?

I've made a promise to myself today, to gain true liberty. I'm going to stop being stubborn about my ways and listen to the voice that loves me and wants me to be free from myself and free from trouble. I am going to give it all up and give way for God to come in. By tonight, just like I have trimmed the bushes in the backyard, I will have trimmed my ego and let it wilt away.

3

The Eternal Flame

An Interview with Jon Everson by Hope Turpin

At the time of this interview Jon Everson was a 27-year-old Bahá'í firefighter in Charlotte, North Carolina. As a firefighter, he came into close contact with many traumatic situations, some of them ending in death. Jon took this opportunity to share with us his views on death and the intricate workings of the soul.

Hope: Firefighters risk their own lives to save the lives and property of others. How do you justify the personal risks to your own life this occupation requires?

Jon: Unfortunately, there are many risks associated with being a firefighter. I have been in very dangerous situations and I'm very thankful to God that I am here to talk about them. Ironically, I do not dwell on these situations or the emotions that I have experienced. Rather, I focus on the happiness that serving others brings to me and the public. This job requires taking calculated risks. The justification of my personal risk is powerfully apparent when I see that a life has been saved!

Hope: The situations you face in the course of your job involve pain, suffering and sometimes even death. How do you deal with the issue of death and dying, as in your profession you encounter it as a matter of course?

Jon: This is a sensitive issue for most firefighters. I cannot even begin to explain the tragedy that I have personally witnessed. It would certainly boggle the mind and perturb the soul. Most firefighters deal with the pain, suffering and death by translating their own disturbed emotions into humor. Humor is a powerful force . . . and it is what we use to deal with these events. Personally speaking, I find comfort in knowing that the physical world is temporary and that the soul is eternal.

Hope: You are a Bahá'í. How does your Faith view the soul?

Jon: As Bahá'ís we view the soul as the inner and essential reality of a human. It is not composed of material matter and it continues to exist after death. The progress of the soul in the next world is contingent upon its deeds in this world. A Bahá'í I know once told me an interesting analogy about the progress of the soul. He said, 'Souls are like rocks that are flung by a slingshot. Most fall short of their target, some get close and still fewer yet actually hit their mark!'

Hope: With death and dying as a regular aspect of your job, it seems obvious to ask what you believe about the path of the soul after death. But I want to ask the reverse: what is the role of the soul here in this lifetime?

Jon: The role of the soul in this lifetime is to know and love God. To be of service to Him and His creation – to do this is true felicity.

Hope: What do you say to someone who has survived a fire when he asks you about someone who has not? How do you help others deal with the issue of death?

Jon: I'm sorry to say that I have never had anyone survive a fire to ask about the remaining victims. Generally speaking, and most certainly in my experience, if one person dies in a fire, so do the remaining occupants. How do I help others deal with the issue of death? I have had very bad experiences with this type of situation. As firefighters we are there to serve, protect and help others but it is important to realize there is a non-emotional factor as well. That is to say, we generally do not know the people we serve, so when tragedy strikes them or their loved ones, we do not have the same level of attachment. Often I will hug or hold the hand of these people and try to console them. Once my engine company was dispatched to a horrific car accident in which a car ran into the back of a semi truck. Miraculously, the young girl driving the car survived but while we were rescuing her from the massively

6

entangled car, her parents happened to drive by the scene of the accident! They rushed out and immediately went into a state of shock and disbelief. That was hard for all of us to see. I was so affected by this that I went to the hospital the next day to spend time with the family.

Hope: How is your own soul impacted when you are successful in saving someone's life? And when you are unable to do so?

Jon: I guess it is all relative. Naturally my soul is stirred when I'm able to help save a life. I find strength in knowing that the soul is eternal! This is an important balance for me. More often than not, we are called to help people in a serious crisis. I'm obedient to God's will.

Hope: Pain and suffering are facts of life but often people wonder how we can have pain and suffering if God is all goodness. How does your faith help you handle your encounters with pain and suffering – physical pain as well as emotional?

Jon: It is true, God is all goodness. Pain and suffering serve to make us stronger. They help us to progress spiritually.

4

Come and Go

Mojan Sami

Do you wake up every morning and remember to take care of
your soul that day? I sure don't. As a matter of fact, I forget my
soul exists until someone reminds me. It just so happens that I was
recently reminded.

Somebody I am close to wants me out of her life. I've only known
her for a year but within that time, she has become a good friend and
like a soul mate. Charming and delightful, she captured the hearts of
all my friends and was immediately an important part of all of their
lives.

A couple of months ago, her world closed in on her. As she
watched her family fall apart, she also fell apart. I saw her pain as she
slowly turned away from all of us. Reluctantly, I became a bystander
as she tried to deny that a calamity had happened to her.

She changed. The fact that I disagreed with her shifting behavior
was not important enough to ruin the friendship but I made the
mistake of telling her anyway. I begged her to take more control
of her life rather than allow her circumstances to control her. My
comments sounded like criticism and the next thing I knew, my dear
friend wanted me out of her life.

My situation is not unique to me – surely, everyone eventually
loses some dearly-loved person. How do we heal after such an afflic-
tion? It is a long and difficult process but we are sure to have grown
when it has passed. It is something that we learn over and over again.
The beginning is always the most painful part and is the hardest on
our souls.

So now I am completely aware of the existence of my soul. It's
as though a piano has been dropped on it. Although I would like
someone to rescue me, I can't seem to find anyone with a shoulder
to cry on. I carry myself over to the next available agent: the Bahá'í

8

writings. The pages don't make great tissues but my soul can sure use the spiritual treasure they offer.

You might be wondering what kind of book changes a person's outlook on life. Have you ever read a mystery novel that kept you entranced through every suspenseful line? Did you feel your heart beating faster the closer the characters got to resolving the mystery? The Bahá'í writings are not novels but the words are so powerful and meaningful – my heart beats faster the closer I come to recognizing the clear solutions that Bahá'u'lláh has given us to apply to our everyday struggles. The Bahá'í writings give me constant joy and inspiration whenever I read them and each time the words have a new way of fitting into that particular stage of my life. The words are refreshing and I find them to be the healing medicine that I have been seeking.

Allow me to point out that I am just an ordinary young woman of 18 years. I have no psychological training and I don't have a license to give prescriptions to anyone in a situation similar to my own. What I have to offer is the inspiration I receive from the Bahá'í writings and the experiences of my everyday life.

When all of this began, I didn't understand how my friend could turn away from the people who cared about her when she needed them most. Instead of questioning this more, I decided the best thing to do was apologize for my behavior and forgive her as well. I don't want to blame her for a broken friendship, nor do I wish to hold a grudge or claim betrayal. I should give her the space she needs. I need to be friendly and my friendliness should be sincere. 'Abdu'l-Bahá says:

> Never speak disparagingly of others, but praise without distinction. Pollute not your tongues by speaking evil of another.[4]

I don't know if our friendship will ever be the same but she knows that my heart is open to her should that time come.

I should also have faith that the predicament will help me, not ail me. I don't want to burn out trying to reverse things; instead, I want to have confidence that the whole situation was meant to be and just accept the Will of God. It is hard to avoid getting caught up in self-pity – it seems like we spend half our lives crying and thinking there is no hope. But hope isn't handed to us on a silver platter. My belief in God and in Bahá'u'lláh allows me to have faith.

> Man is under all conditions immersed in a sea of God's blessings. Therefore, be thou not hopeless under any circumstances, but rather be firm in thy hope.[5]

Feeling hopeless never has any benefits.

Lastly, I need to prevent my emotions from interfering with my goals and duties. Emotions aren't bad – they help make us unique individuals and expressing them can be very healthy for our well-being. However, used in the wrong way, our emotions can be harmful. Detaching oneself from a situation, as I am attempting to do with this one, keeps one's mind clear. Rather than being absorbed by my pain, I can choose to tend to it by *not* occupying myself with it. Detachment is not the same as pretending things are okay – it is believing that they are.

> Life is a load which must be carried on while we are on earth, but the cares of the lower things of life should not be allowed to monopolize all the thoughts and aspirations of a human being.[6]

Detachment is one of the handiest tools in my healing process, difficult as it is to achieve. The best part? It can be integrated into any and every experience, allowing the same piano that crushed my soul to help me make music.

Having friends is one of the great bounties of living; losing them is one of the hardest. Will I ever again have a soul mate like the one I lost? I can't answer that. As a matter of fact, I don't think anyone can. But I can tell you one thing – find your soul medicine, put it on the top shelf of your soul cabinet, and remember that your soul needs the greatest care. When the time comes that you need to let go of someone important to you, you'll know to take two doses of your soul medicine and call me in the morning.

5

Soul Reason

An Interview with Charity Pabst by Oceana Brandon

Charity Elise Pabst was born in Banners Ferry, Idaho, a tiny town just 30 miles south of Canada. At the time of this interview she was 22 years old and lived with her parents and brother in Portland, Maine, where she was in her final year at the University of Southern Maine studying for a Bachelor of Fine Arts in ceramics. Charity planned to do a period of service for the Bahá'í Faith after graduating. She was also interested in learning more about the Montessori method of education. I spoke with her about her experiences with art and education and about souls in the next world.

Oceana: Why are you interested in the Montessori method of teaching?

Charity: I love children and I'm very interested in education. I volunteered at a Montessori school for about four months a couple of years ago and that was a really good experience. I'm not particularly interested in participating in the education system of this country, the way it is right now.

Oceana: Like public schools?

Charity: I'm more interested in alternative methods of education. I love the Montessori method because the emphasis is on learning in natural ways.

Oceana: What experiences in your life have contributed to your views about schooling?

Charity: I went to a public school here in Maine until I was 15. I feel like I was always very lucky. Whatever creativity or enthusiasm I had was recognized when I was young. Throughout elementary school I was in a program called Project Exploration, a special class intended for 'gifted and talented children'. But then again, a program for gifted and talented children? What is that? It proved to be a good outlet for me but what did it mean to all of the other kids, who were 'gifted and talented' in other ways? I guess that is why I am interested in the Montessori method and other alternative methods of education: they encourage the creative capacities latent in all children. Now, junior high, that was a difficult time. I don't know if that was because of the specific school I attended or if it was just a really tough age. Maybe both.

Oceana: When I was in junior high, it seemed that the social experience, rather than just the schooling, made it such a difficult time. Everyone's changing and growing.

Charity: Peer pressure at that point is very strong. I didn't really care about boys but because it was expected that everyone should be interested in relationships, suddenly I became interested. Or maybe I pretended. It was really confusing.

Oceana: So where did you go at age 15?

Charity: I went to a public school for my freshman year. It's pretty much a blur to me. Maybe I was still recovering from the trauma of middle school. After my freshman year, I participated in a youth institute at Green Acre Bahá'í School and I saw a presentation about the Maxwell International Bahá'í School, which had just begun that year. I got really excited about it and told my parents. They were encouraging, so I applied, was accepted and went three weeks later. That's where I spent the rest of high school. I was in the first graduating class.

Oceana: Is your whole family Bahá'í?

Charity: I've grown up in a Bahá'í family but the Bahá'í Faith is something I've had to find for myself. Even though I grew up within the Bahá'í community, knowing a lot of Bahá'ís and being familiar with the principles, the Faith wasn't an integral part of my life all along.

Oceana: How did attending Maxwell increase your enthusiasm for the Bahá'í Faith?

Charity: At Maxwell the Bahá'í Faith was the focus of everything we did. I was away from home, distanced from my normal life, with the opportunity to see things from a different perspective. A number of things transpired during my time at Maxwell, such that a love for the Bahá'í Faith and for Bahá'u'lláh was kindled in my heart.

Oceana: When you leave family, you're almost forced to find yourself. You have to survive and be your own person.

Charity: I never thought my parents pressured me to be a Bahá'í but I think they had hopes and aspirations for me. Even if they tried their utmost not to project that onto me, it was there and particularly at that age.

Oceana: After your graduation from Maxwell, you went to Samoa. Why did you go?

Charity: I was going to college part time then. I had begun some classes in the spring when plans for my trip started to materialize. It's a long story. It seemed like the right thing to do, so I dropped all of my classes and went to do a few months of volunteer service. I was there for about four months and lived with two different families. There is a Bahá'í Montessori school on the grounds of the Bahá'í House of Worship and I worked there every day. That was a nice period of service. It gave me a different perspective on my life.

Oceana: Once you get some distance from something, you gain a better perspective on it.

Charity: I agree. Sometimes it's helpful when that can be a physical distance. I returned home from Samoa and the following year I began college full time.

Oceana: In Samoa you had new cultural experiences and an example of the Montessori method. Would you spend time in another country teaching at a Montessori school?

Charity: I'm not sure. I'm interested in the Montessori method because its themes and ideals are fascinating. I really love its holistic, balanced approach to education, encouraging children to grow and develop in ways they're interested in, rather than pushing things onto them. The Montessori program is universal. It's recognized in this country and elsewhere as well. I'm also really interested in the idea of an orphanage.

Oceana: I'd like to ask you about your artwork because you do some really amazing paintings and drawings. Have you always been into art?

Charity: Yes. I have always been interested in art and drawing but I never took it that seriously. I had a really powerful experience when I was 17. A good friend of mine was an incredible artist. I always admired her work and she encouraged me a lot. When I was 17, she passed away. It was a really, really hard time for me for a number of months. It was a saga of grief and of not understanding why it happened. I tried to relate to where she was after she died. As I went through my own healing process, coming to understand that our souls are very much connected and that she is probably closer to me now than she ever was before, I found this increasing thirst to be actively making art. As I did that, I developed technically. I had an abundance of ideas. I feel that it had a lot to do with her passing and helping me from the next world. She had a big effect on me and inspired me to make art. She really feeds my creativity.

Oceana: So the passing of your friend made you think of your relationship in a new way.

Charity: I felt so lonely and left behind. This person was my best friend and I didn't see why she was taken like that in the first place. At the time, it was very hard for me to understand.

Oceana: Some of your paintings include figures that look like souls ascending. Some of the more abstract ones make me think of moving from one dimension to another. Did you intend that?

Charity: I am definitely aware of that, particularly because my own art began to flourish when this theme of the relationship between souls was in my consciousness. I have thought about it very much and prayed about it. It became part of my creative process, so it came out more intuitively. I'm not always good at articulating in words those kinds of relationships. That's why I paint and make things with clay.

Oceana: What deeper understanding did you gain about the spiritual reality of souls?

Charity: I went through a long period when I was thinking and thinking, trying to understand in my mind what was going on. You know, 'Wherever you are, do you still love me, and I need to know that you didn't leave me behind and you're gone.' I was really grappling with that. I needed to know that I was still dear to this person who was so dear to me in this life. I finally had to stop thinking about it with my own limited intellect. I became detached. I gave in to whatever my mind was trying to figure out and reached a new level of understanding with my heart and maybe with my own soul. When I could lift the veils from my mind's understanding, there was a much more profound understanding with my heart and that was my real understanding.

When I came to this point, when I felt that we were still very close, closer, in fact, than we had been before, I had a vision of a painting that someday I would love to do. I can imagine it – or maybe I can just feel it more than I can imagine it, because I have no idea how to put it down on the canvas. I have a picture of when I pass from this life and ascend to the next world of our souls reuniting with one another – these two beings of energy, like light. She's waiting for me, somewhere, or she will be when I'm coming – these two balls of energy, two forces of light, coming together and intertwining and ascending together. The feeling I imagine is such joy and pleasure at being together again. It's very light-filled and the feeling is one of extreme happiness. Now that I have that to think of, it's a comfort to me. I feel like I know that this will happen.

It's hard to think about things like this because I've obviously never experienced anything like this before. It's not tangible. How can we possibly attempt to fathom this reality that is so different from what we physically know? I guess it's always on my mind, in my heart.

6

Millennium

An Interview with Rachel Gargiulo by Santina Vu

Rachel: I live in Brunswick, Maine. I'm 16 years old and a senior in high school. I spent my sophomore year at Maxwell International Bahá'í School, which is up in Vancouver, Canada. It was incredible. It was a time when I really had the chance to grow and change. After that, I came back to Brunswick to live with my family and spent my junior year there. I'm planning to go to Africa for a year of service with a friend of mine.

Santina: What was your life like growing up as a child?

Rachel: I lived in Connecticut for a while. We were a quarter of a mile back in the woods. We lived in a little log cabin. I remember going on walks with my father through the woods when I was little. There were all kinds of old cars and a school bus and things like that. That fascinated me. There were ducks – we had a little pond – and goats. We lived on sort of a little farm. Then we moved to New York and I went to a Catholic school for a year so I could learn to read. My parents thought I would learn better at a Catholic school rather than at a public school. I had my little sister to play with and pick on. We had lots of fun. We used to play dress-up and things like that. I don't remember being unhappy for any reason. I was usually pretty content.

Santina: What sort of tests and difficulties did you experience?

Rachel: When I was at Maxwell, it was difficult for me to share my space with other people. I was used to having a pretty big room to myself. At Maxwell I had to share a room about the same size with other people. It was really hard to learn that I wasn't as good a person as I thought. I had to deal with issues like racism, which is inherent in our society. Maxwell was a very different environ-

16

ment and I took more notice of the way I was feeling. I had a very hard time realizing that there were things I had to overcome. As Bahá'ís, we have to go against the mainstream flow of what most other people are doing. That is a big test for me because I get sucked into it sometimes, just like everyone else.

Santina: How did being at Maxwell shape your character?

Rachel: I think I've been able to develop my strengths more, as a result of finding out more about myself. When my friends are having problems and I sit down and talk with them, I'm able to give them advice and I'm also able to give them a positive energy that maybe they don't get anywhere else, even in their families.

Santina: What's most important to you?

Rachel: Definitely the aid of Bahá'u'lláh. Where else can I get what I'm looking for, anything that I need, anything that I want? It all comes from Bahá'u'lláh. I don't always know what I need, so it definitely comes from Him. The Bahá'í Faith and the Covenant too. It's so important to stay strong in the Covenant because that's the origin of everything else that comes through you, the origin of all the qualities and all the positive energy that passes through you to other people. We're told in the Bahá'í writings that our strength is the power of the Covenant and nothing else.

Santina: Why do you think that is?

Rachel: If you look around society, you can see that things are falling apart very rapidly. They're not what they used to be. A lot of people don't know why it's happening. It's because of the break-down of relationships. The Bahá'í writings speak of tests and difficulties to come and I think that part of that is the breakdown of relationships that people are experiencing. We're told in the writings how to make these relationships work.

Santina: Tell me how your Bahá'í principles have helped you to solve problems or help a friend.

Rachel: When I came back to Maine and started my junior year back at my old high school, with all of the people I knew from before, a couple of my friends were having a really difficult time with their families. I found that through reading what the writings say about Bahá'í family life and relationships, I was able to give them advice or just lend a helping hand with the principles that I know.

Santina: How do you generally feel about your day when you get up in the morning?

Rachel: When I first wake up in the morning, I generally feel very positive about it. I try to say 'Alláh-u-Abhá' ('God is Most Glorious') as the first thing I do. That gives me a really good feel for the rest of the day. Sometimes it doesn't go the way I was hoping it would but that doesn't mean it was bad.

Santina: Are there things that you wish were different about the world or in your own life?

Rachel: Lots of things. I'm happy with a lot of the things in my life. I think I'm very fortunate because many people aren't happy with even their own lives. The world around me needs a lot of help. I try to give that help. During the day I find that it's really easy to have a positive effect on people.

Santina: What do you think your life will be like in ten years?

Rachel: I'm open to anything! In ten years, I hope to be through college and have a job. I really love Canada and I'd like to live there. I want to teach English as a second language – something I could do in another country also. I hope to be spending a lot of time away from the United States to get a feel for the rest of the world.

Santina: How do you feel about the state of the world today?

Rachel: It's constantly changing, for one thing. In general, part of it is crumbling and that's the society that we can see around us but also a good part is being built. As Bahá'ís, we're building up something else underneath the decaying part of society. We're building a foundation for people to turn to when the old world order crumbles. Very soon, we're going to see a lot of changes in the way things are run, in the way people run their lives, even the way they think about things.

Santina: What will the world be like in 20 years?

Rachel: We're told in the Bahá'í writings that we'll have the Lesser Peace, which might be only a few years away. The Lesser Peace starts with governments, with people from all around the world pulling together. I think that we're going to have to work from there. In 20 years we should be able to make some good progress. I think that there will be fewer incidents of racism and that people will be able to pull together much more easily. We're coming up with incredible new ways of communicating. Not so long ago, telegraphs and telephones were invented. Now you can talk to anyone in the world over your computer. It's getting so much easier to communicate. The world is getting smaller and smaller.

Santina: How do you think your life will be affected by all the changes of the new millennium?

Rachel: Probably positively. There will be a lot of changes and there's no way to tell just what those changes will be. In the new millennium, a lot of things will be difficult but there will be more Bahá'ís to work with and more friends of the Faith.

Santina: How will things be better then?

Rachel: Many people are becoming more familiar with the writings of Bahá'u'lláh, the Báb, 'Abdu'l-Bahá and Shoghi Effendi – the writings of the Bahá'í Faith and its principles. A lot of people are recognizing, hey, that's what I need, that's what I've been looking for all this time. We learn in those writings that if we follow the Covenant and we try our hardest, that's the most important thing. What matters is the effort we put into it. If we do that, it will be easier and easier for us to understand things and play those understandings out in our everyday lives.

7

The Path

Erika Hastings

The future completely obsesses us from the moment we are born. Even before we start school, people ask us what we want to be when we grow up, as if that will determine our success in life. From the time we are six years old, we are taught that if we become a doctor or a lawyer, we will be financially secure and therefore happy. Money becomes the focus and primary reason for educational success, even at such a young age.

Students subsequently go to school not to learn but to be able to enjoy a good career in the future; hence the moral and spiritual aspects of an educational experience are deemed unimportant. Subconsciously, the drive to acquire money affects us all, even at the expense of our spirituality.

Three years ago I was treading this path of supposed success, pursuing a career in the medical field. I knew I wanted to work with people and be of service to humanity and what could be better than saving lives? After I graduated from high school, I decided to go to Honduras for a year of volunteer service at a small hospital to gain real-life experience.

During my year of service, I realized that I did not want to work in medicine for the rest of my life. I was quite torn up about it and felt that I had to immediately make the single decision which would supposedly determine my eternal fate.

I recently learned that on average, people change their careers at least four or five times. Knowing earlier that it is acceptable or even common to change careers would have helped me in my struggle. I didn't expect then to have the opportunity to explore a number of different career options and I didn't know that any given option wasn't final.

I was working one day with the director of the hospital and shared my anxiety over making this decision. She told me that the most important thing was for me to be happy about what I was doing. 'If you are happy in your work,' she said, 'then no matter what you do, you will be able to serve humanity to an unimaginably great extent.'

In my effort to remain happy during difficult situations, my entire attitude has changed and I am honestly enjoying life a lot more. This is one of the greatest pieces of advice I ever received, possibly because it's what I wanted to hear in the first place. I wanted someone to speak for happiness and tell to me that *it* is the priority.

After my year in Honduras, I decided to attend university and study what I really love: art and languages. I am one of the few people I know who actually enjoys studying at a university – and it is because I enjoy the subject matter.

I have discovered still more ways to grow and change on this new path. I used to be a compulsive planner, especially of my future. Then one year, somehow everything I had planned for my summer work fell on its face. I arrived home for the summer rather late in the season. I needed a job but nothing was available. This meant that I had to put into practice my two least favorite virtues: patience and detachment. The funny thing is, when I am working on these two, especially trusting in God that everything will work out, it always does. The night I got home, I received a call offering me a job on a fishing boat in Alaska. A week later, there I was, on the boat.

While I was in Alaska, I witnessed a very serious accident. A co-worker fell two stories down an elevator shaft onto hard cement. Fortunately he only broke his wrist but at the time – looking down on him from above – we all thought he was dead, or close to it. That experience made me stop and rethink my purpose in life. Over and over I thought, 'That could have been me.' I realized how close we truly are to death. What, then, is the purpose of our lives? It is through the acquisition of virtues and service to humanity that we can, however minutely, better understand and serve our Creator. In my case, it's time for me to get busy working on the virtues of detachment and patience.

I am enjoying my studies and I am working on acquiring virtues – but all the same, it will probably be difficult for me to find work when I graduate. That brings me back to the question of happiness versus material success. In our society, with so much emphasis on materialism, it is easy for our priorities to fall out of line. What kind of a success is a person if she makes a lot of money but has no friends and her family life is falling apart?

Resisting the pressure to achieve only material success is, I feel, one of the most powerful tools we possess, offering endless opportunities for growth and change – forms of spiritual success. This is the path I wish to follow.

8

Lens of Hope

An Interview with Josh Lincoln by Dan Makoski

Josh: I was born in Forest Park, Illinois. My parents moved to France about a year and a half after I was born and then later moved to the Central African Republic, to Cameroon and then to the Ivory Coast. I came back to the US to go to school. After high school I spent a year of volunteer service at the Bahá'í World Centre in Haifa, Israel, working as a security guard. Then I went to college at Georgetown University in Washington DC and came here to Massachusetts to graduate school at Tufts University in Medford. I got married eleven months ago. Things are going well. Right now I'm working on a PhD.

Dan: What was your undergraduate major?

Josh: International Affairs.

Dan: Did you focus within your major?

Josh: My focus was on international law and international organization; that is, the UN system. I also did a lot of work on West Africa, North Africa and the Middle East.

Dan: What was your focus for your Master's degree?

Josh: Negotiation, conflict resolution and international organization. For my PhD, I'm studying nationalism, identity and ethnicity, which is all about how different groups get along in society.

Dan: What application do you see for this area of study?

Josh: Often it is very theoretical to start with but it's important to inform theory with practice and vice versa. A lot of people work specifically on the economic programs of different countries, developing a relationship between two states or between a state and the UN.

Dan: Give us an example of your work in this area.

Josh: In a very humble capacity, I worked for a non-governmental organization – a NGO – this summer, which was trying to forward the mediation process between Liberian civil war factions. It was really, really hard to do. It made a lot of sense conceptually but when people have been killing each other's children, wives and husbands, mediation is a very complex thing to achieve.

Dan: What do you see happening in the years to come? Tell me your view of this crazy world.

Josh: A lot of stuff is happening simultaneously and sometimes it's very hard to distinguish one pattern from another. You can't figure out if a particular event is part of the old world system being rolled up or the new system being put down. Is this part of integration or is it part of disintegration? We're in a period of transition. Periods of transition are inherently unstable. If you put a pot of water on the stove, the water changes to steam through boiling. Boiling is a very, very unstable state. We have a lot of different things going around, bubbling all over the place.

Dan: Many people might argue there is no process of integration. Is there a difference in magnitude between these two processes?

Josh: All the negative stuff is usually what makes the headlines. There are positive things happening but the negative things are more dramatic. The positive things are usually more progressive and subtle. In the 20th century we had two world wars, with probably the largest number of people ever killed in the history of the world. At the same time, we've seen the evolution of a global society and a lot of experimenting with international institutions. After World War I, in 1919, Woodrow Wilson and other statesmen established the League of Nations. Many people were totally ecstatic; they thought that world peace had arrived. Right after World War I, after the signing of the Treaty of Versailles, 'Abdu'l-Bahá cautioned everybody, saying that the hearts of men were still smoldering even as their lips spoke of peace. The League of Nations, the first embryonic world organization, had within it the seeds of disappointment. It developed some ideas of how to get nations to work together. Then it failed at one point. The Second World War and the United Nations followed, which was the return of international cooperation. All the states and people working on that had their own prejudices. In 1945 most of Africa was still a colony of some empire or another. Nonetheless, the UN has continued to evolve and all the elements of a future world society have been growing slowly, going through experimentation phases. That doesn't make for hot news and there's no denying the ugly stuff – there's roughly between 30 and 35 major armed conflicts going on today. For most of the people of the world, it's a terrible time. The fact that you and I may not feel it directly is because we're sitting in a very lucky place. We have food on the table and there's no war going on in the street.

Dan: It's good to get that perspective. So we need to equip ourselves with a certain type of lens to view world affairs.

Josh: I think we have to train ourselves, particularly as youth, to develop the habits of reading newspapers, listening to the radio, checking the Web, so we're aware of what's going on around us. Shoghi Effendi read a lot of newspapers and kept up on world affairs. He was in Haifa, Israel, building the Bahá'í gardens and shrines on Mount Carmel by day, writing *God Passes By* by night, with World War II raging around him, corresponding with every Bahá'í community in the world, and he'd still get up in the morning and read *The Times* of London, the *Jerusalem Post* and the *Herald Tribune* and he'd cut articles out and put them in files. If the Guardian could do that, then it's probably something we should do as well.

Dan: Some people don't do this because it depresses them to keep up with world politics. How can you protect yourself from a negative perspective, while still informing yourself about what's going on in the world?

Josh: I do get depressed sometimes. We need to be aware of what's going on and at the same time not confuse that with what we need to do. We need to understand the world's events but not engage in partisan politics and instead focus on personal spiritual growth. You get up in the morning and read the newspapers but do it after you pray and read the sacred writings.

Dan: So you have to get your spiritual food first. That's the lens that will allow you to see correctly.

Josh: Yeah! When you get up in the morning, you can read a passage from the sacred writings and then sit down and read the newspaper or listen to the radio and think, 'How do I understand this event in light of what I read this morning?' Don't let it drag you down because that's one less person that the rest of us can count on. It's important to stay spiritually detached from the incredible chaos of the world and instead to focus on our own spiritual growth.

Dan: The main paradigm operating in world affairs asserts that we are living in a state of anarchy, conditioned upon state sovereignty being the highest form of legitimate authority in the world. What do you see in the next several years regarding this?

Josh: The doctrine of state sovereignty says that states are supreme. If one state decides to do something, there's nothing anyone can do to stop it and no one can tell the state to stop. You can make a good case that state sovereignty is gradually becoming an obsolete doctrine. When you look at all the international agreements that states have – agreements on trade, treaties of friendship, agreements to help one another in the event of security problems, environmental treaties – each one limits sovereignty. This is now the accepted way of working, which really means that absolute sovereignty is no longer an issue.

Dan: There's a quotation at the beginning of *Turning Point for All Nations*, a statement of the Bahá'í International Community, in which Shoghi Effendi says that sovereignty is a fetish which states must give up.

Josh: The Guardian also talks about the effects of nationalism if carried to excess. He talks about sane patriotism, which is basically a healthy form of love for one's country and which should not be confused with excessive, bigoted nationalism. There's a lot of bigoted nationalism going on out there today. I'm particularly interested in how majority groups get along with minority groups – that is, large groups in one society getting along with smaller groups of a different race, background, culture or even language. This is probably the single most important issue for the future. The pivotal principle of the Bahá'í Faith is the unity of all humanity. As Bahá'ís, we often talk about this as if it's a nice, pretty little thing, maybe without understanding its impact. This principle is about international affairs. It's about Serbs getting along with Croats in Yugoslavia, it's about the Hutus and the Tutsis getting along in Rwanda and Burundi. It's really very, very deep. We are just beginning to learn how to handle it. If my people and your people share a river, how do we decide who gets to use the water and whether your use of the water is going to detract from my use of it? Our earth is already so small now that we have to learn how to share its resources and live together very closely. That's very challenging. When Bahá'u'lláh says the pivotal principle is unity, it's going to be the single most important element, I think, in the way individuals and states live together. That's the future.

Dan: Some people pass that off as being idealistic. How can unity be so powerful as to correct all of the imperfections we see now?

Josh: The Lesser Peace involves the political unity of the states of the world. It does not mean absolute unity – it means some form of agreement on a purely political level. Once the Lesser Peace is established, we will move towards the Most Great Peace and deal with spiritual questions.

Dan: So we're talking about the political unity of the world. When?

Josh: Sometimes we think of the Lesser Peace as an event as opposed to a process. We could already be witnessing the Lesser Peace. Nations increasingly agree on how to solve our problems.

Dan: What do you see in that process?

Josh: The Lesser Peace is only the first of several stages that will take us to the Most Great Peace. We know that the Lesser Peace itself will be gradual. There are two things going on, what Shoghi Effendi calls the twin processes of integration and disintegration. There are wars, problems, conflicts; and on the other hand, there are new institutions, ideas, debates, resolutions and groups of people getting together around certain issues. Everything that's happening now has a reason for it. It's a big collective learning process.

Dan: A lot of people expect that something good will occur only after something really terrible happens.

Josh: A single cataclysmic event could totally shock the world into a new realization. The calamity is actually happening now. We, sitting here in North America, may not see it because we're in the top two percent of the wealthiest of the world's population. We're insulated by three or four thousand miles of ocean. What's more is our news doesn't tell us the extent of everyone else's suffering. We see little glimpses of world leaders getting together but that's not the reality of what's happening in the rest of the world. Sixty-five to 75 per cent of the world's population is living in hell for lack of food, lack of jobs, lack of security, war, conflict, disease – you name it. There is suffering at an incredible level. Shoghi Effendi said that the Lesser Peace will be like establishing a body without a spirit – a mechanism, an initial structural setup, that will be filled with spiritual substance later. That substance is where the Bahá'í community will be directly involved – it will not play an active role in the coming of the Lesser Peace. The Bahá'í writings say that the states of the world will draw upon the Bahá'í principles and ideals without knowing it. You can see it now, in the equality of men and women, the need for a universal language or aspects of world government. If you go to the UN any day of the week, they're talking about one of the principles of the Bahá'í Faith. It's only after the Lesser Peace that the Bahá'í community will play a vital, direct role, infusing spirit into the structure.

Dan: So the role of religion in this process is not only important but it's almost the source?

Josh: Yes, in the second stage. The first stage, the Lesser Peace, is like a bunch of people who are jogging, running out of air so fast that they finally agree amongst themselves to stop running. Once everyone stops, they can begin to consult on where to move that makes the most sense. That is the beginning of the journey to the Most Great Peace, where spiritual matters become incredibly important.

Dan: Since the fall of communism, people have had a sense that capitalism is victorious, that the end of history has occurred and it's only the process of steady democratization that will lead to economic peace.

Josh: When communism failed in 1989 – when the Berlin Wall came down – everyone said, 'You see? Communism disintegrated internally, therefore capitalism is the system of choice.' That's pretty faulty logic. The one doesn't imply the other. If one can disintegrate internally, it suggests that the other could as well. Capitalism as an economic and social system doesn't meet our needs. It's a great system for making and spending money but it doesn't account for the fact that we're spiritual beings, that we have needs to be met in that sense and that we have a responsibility for one another as spiritual beings. That's one of the reasons why life for Bahá'í youth is so challenging.

Dan: What about the youth? What about the grass roots stirring of the energy of youth now and beyond?

Josh: It's an extremely special time. It's also rough. Being a youth these days is, on the one hand, a great privilege but the privilege comes at a price, based on a challenge. The challenge in North America is that it's a really materialistic place. There are a lot of challenges to building one's spiritual side, individually, to a point where it's strong enough to handle the world as it spins around you. I think the youth today are more qualified than ever before to build the new world order. More than any generation before, they have a grasp of the meaning of the word 'diversity'. The communications revolution, the Internet, all these things – they increase our understanding of how beautiful the world is in its complexity. Youth can give tremendous service to their community at large, with an understanding of their own spiritual beings as well as of the world around them.

Dan: Besides an appreciation of diversity and the perspective of our global village, what are some other skills that you think it would be wise for youth to focus on?

Josh: Having a good grasp of language and writing is really important. There's no substitute for it in this world. Everything we do, every way we serve our Bahá'í communities, is dependent on our ability to communicate. Working on that is pretty important.

Dan: This brings up the question of hope. There's very little of it out there. Why would someone have hope?

Josh: There isn't much hope out there. Why do we Bahá'ís have hope for the future? We're not exclusively concerned with how far our bodies will go on this earth because we understand that our soul transcends this world and will continue to live through all the worlds of God. Also, we have hope because Bahá'u'lláh tells us that we should. Shoghi Effendi said that the immediate future is distressingly dark but he also said that the distant future is gloriously brilliant. It's a matter of faith. We have to realize that humanity has come this far and the growth of humanity will continue.

9

The Culture of College

An Interview with Shagha Moghaddam by Kate Knaplund

Shagha, 20, was a university student who had just finished her second-year final exams when she spoke with me.

Kate: How would you define pop culture?

Shagha: Well, I don't think it's one specific culture. In the United States you can find many different pop cultures. But it's basically the culture that younger people and students live by. It's defined by the clothes they wear, the things they do for hobbies, by hanging out, by fun, by what they're most engaged in every day, by the kind of music they listen to, the sounds they listen to. It's not constant – it changes every few years.

Kate: Have college students created a culture within the American culture?

Shagha: I definitely think so. I think that college students have a sub-culture in the United States. I can only give my view of my own university. There, college students have almost made a bubble where they live themselves. We have many people from different parts of the world – international students. But they seem pretty uniform. You'll find a group of people from, say, Asia, China, Japan. You have groups of Latinos, African-Americans and white Americans. They're grouped off and they each seem to have their own sub-culture. But there's an overall culture of college students. It's a generalization – but it's parties, drinking, going to clubs or frat parties – partying and drinking seem to exist across all the groups. There are, of course, exceptions. There are also very studious people who stay away from all that and keep to their books.

Kate: How do the ideas, values and what is popular with the college students fit into American pop culture?

Shagha: I think if you look at American culture, the way people fit into society, it's more real life. College is not the real world. I find many people at the university who I feel – I'm not trying to be judgmental – but I feel are not living in the real world at all. They seem unaware of real-life issues and world issues. So maybe in that way student culture doesn't really fit in, or it conflicts in many ways with the overall American culture. The students don't seem to be very aware of world issues or things that are important. For example, racism. Many students at my university don't even think about racism, depending on which group you speak to. The people who fit into the minority groups in the US are a lot more aware of it. But other students seem not to be aware of it at all. It has to come up. As a Bahá'í, for example, you have to force yourself to be conscious of it every day because it can get so lost at college.

Kate: Is it hard at college to live by Bahá'í standards?

Shagha: Well, there are a lot of aspects of college culture which conflict with Bahá'í standards, for example, drinking and promiscuity. It seems that people are much more promiscuous and they have more sexual relationships with random people in college. You meet someone one time and that's it, you don't see him again. It's very random and not very selective. People don't usually have just one partner, they have many partners. So that aspect conflicts with Bahá'í standards of chastity and abstinence from drinking. Sometimes I go out with my friends who drink and do this and that but they all know that I don't do it. They don't even ask me to drink. I say, 'No, I don't. I don't agree with that.' But they also know that they have a choice between doing it or not.

It's very important which friends I make. I'm attracted to some people who I don't know at all and then I end up becoming friends with them. I learn about them and discover they're very similar to myself in moral ways. Many of the friends I've made, we start talking and I learn that they have a lot of the same standards as I do as a Bahá'í. It's important to make those friends. You have to have a balance.

Kate: You were living at home for a while. Going from a home to the city – is it much of a difference?

Shagha: It's actually very different. Going to college, I'm on my own, more independent. My parents raised me at home and taught me certain things. When I went to college, finally everything I'd been taught and everything I believed in was put to a real test because I was completely on my own. Most of the time when I'm at home I just go to my parents. At college I ask myself, can I do it on my own? Can I hold onto my values, my manners and all those things, on my own? I think that for Bahá'í youth being at college is the most important time to stay within the Bahá'í community, maybe more than any other time in our lives. I think some people drift away from the Bahá'í Faith; they don't go to Feast anymore. So before we go to college, it's important to get into the habit of obligatory prayer and things like that because when we get to college, without that foundation, it's very difficult to build it. But that's the time when you need it the most!

Kate: Are there many Bahá'ís to help you out at college?

Shagha: In this city there are a lot of other colleges and many Bahá'í students. In the next city there are a lot of Bahá'í youth. I go to Feast and the Bahá'í Center. On campus, we have other Bahá'ís but some aren't active at all, so I never see them. Every college differs. Some colleges don't have any Bahá'ís; at others there are many.

Kate: In my school, each group has a different culture. For example, the guys have one thing, the girls have another thing and if you travel a hundred miles north it will be a different thing again. If you wear the same jeans or the same shirt and if you don't get new clothes that are nice and pretty, people notice and put their nose up in your face. Does that happen at college?

Shagha: That happens a lot less at college. I think people care less but I think that may be because of their maturity. I think in junior high school and high school, people enter that stage where they're very aware of their bodies. It's almost at an extreme. It's very, very important at that age. But I think as you get older it becomes less and less important. But it still is a big thing what kind of clothes you wear. A lot of wealthy students go to my university. People drive their BMWs. Some people make fun of that at the university but there are a lot who try to do it – you know, have retro clothing. Some students are always shopping; a lot of them are very wealthy. But I think it depends on who you surround yourself with, the kind of friends you make. That's what's really going to affect you most. That's why I say it's very important to make good friends and not be superficial. But more importantly, people look at who you are. Of course you will find people who are very superficial and who just care about money and the kind of car you drive, the kind of clothes you wear and all those sorts of things. But there are also the same number of people who do care about who you are inside and that's a lot more important. That really does shine through.

10

Reflections from the Holy Land

Carrie Smith

Every day for the past 18 months I've wakened to the melodious singing of nightingales on Mount Carmel and have risen to serve Bahá'u'lláh. After serving for so long, as I get out of my warm bed and gaze out the window that overlooks the Mediterranean Sea, I feel compelled to reflect on my experiences here. I ask myself, in meditation, if I have served the Universal House of Justice to my fullest capacity. As I meditate, all my fears and joys from the days and months gone by come to the surface.

As these emotions of inadequacy, regret, achievement, appreciation and gratitude envelop my whole being, I ask myself why I'm here, who am I to be here and why did the only infallible institution in the world invite me to serve on God's holiest mountain? There is only one obvious answer – because God loves me right along with the rest of humanity.

So now I'm sobbing and tears are running down my face as I realize this once again. But then I ask Bahá'u'lláh why He loves me. I'm sitting on my bed, dumbfounded and crying, so out of control that I can hardly breathe, facing 'Akká, the city where Bahá'u'lláh was imprisoned for more than 20 years.

Then I begin to think. I think out loud. I think quietly and reverently about how I have lived my life. My thoughts replay each day of my life here and I see them as the most precious opportunities for service I've ever had the privilege of fulfilling. I can't help but feel a sense of emptiness, however, a sense of loss for the opportunities I missed before coming here. Those opportunities will never return. The time has come and gone.

My sense of loss stems from the notion that I may not have seized every opportunity to teach the Cause of Bahá'u'lláh before coming here and on the day of reckoning I will have to answer to Him for neglecting His most precious Cause. For Bahá'ís, teaching the Bahá'í Faith is seen as the most meritorious of all deeds in the sight of God and teaching the Faith in Israel has not been allowed since the time of Bahá'u'lláh's residence in the Holy Land.

Our purpose for living on this material realm, as I understand the Bahá'í writings, is to know and to love God, and we do that by first teaching the Bahá'í Faith to ourselves through deepening, prayer, meditation and living the life. Then, we come to know God by sharing His message with others, and through this exercise, we come to know more about ourselves and about our own spiritual attributes, which reflect the attributes of God. If we don't do this – if we are inactive – then it is as though we were dead and this is the most horrible cruelty we could inflict upon ourselves.

This material life is like living in the mother's womb where the fetus grows and develops into an infant. When all of its faculties are complete, the infant passes through the birth canal into the next plane of existence. Our soul's purpose for living in this material realm is to develop spiritual strengths, through the knowledge of God, to use in the next life, in the spiritual realm. The Bahá'í writings elucidate that humans are not physically reincarnated. Rather, at the moment of death, our soul continues to live in the next realm while our body decays here on earth.

In light of current events, my own actions seem more valuable than ever in terms of meeting the demands of living a true Bahá'í life and teaching the Bahá'í Faith to others. Right now, while living on Mount Carmel, I can deepen in the writings of the three central figures of our beloved Cause. But once I leave, only God knows what will happen.

Dearly beloved brothers and sisters, you are free! Take this moment and live in this moment, for it will never return. So many of you are already out there in the field doing your part. But when Bahá'u'lláh is calling upon us to wake up, who is He talking to? He's talking to the faces who claim His name but play the wrong game.

It is true that the Cause will triumph over all obstacles whether or not we arise to serve because His coming is the promise of all ages. But we must continually endeavor to deepen ourselves in the writings no matter how much it hurts – because the true seekers are waiting for us. They are attentively waiting to hear the message of Bahá'u'lláh and to witness the unity of humankind with their own eyes!

Two years ago I was in Chicago participating in a Bahá'í institute course. I would use the subway train to travel back and forth from one end of town to the other. One day I was sitting on train waiting for its departure when a youth climbed aboard and, in a rush, asked me if she was on the right train. She was.

After a sigh of relief, she began to ask questions: where was I from, how long had I been in Chicago, and so on. At this time my mind was really not thinking about teaching the Faith, as everything seemed to be so abrupt. Without even thinking about how to respond to her questions, I began to teach the Faith by explaining what had brought me to Chicago. Not even five minutes had passed before I could see the burning light in her eyes as I told her about the basic principles of our Faith. Not even the foreign name of Bahá'u'lláh discouraged her appetite for more.

I could see hope radiating from her whole being. I too felt the excitement of the moment. My blood pressure went up, my heart raced, my soul was riveted by the experience – I had to hold back the tears. Never before had anyone been so receptive to my efforts to teach the Faith.

We exchanged phone numbers, kept in touch, became friends. After a while she attended firesides and met other Bahá'í youth. Because of an unexpected move I had to leave Chicago and was unable to stay in contact with her but I will never forget that first encounter. Many of us have similar stories. Imagine how happy Bahá'u'lláh would be if all of the Bahá'í youth could share these stories amongst His children.

Having that experience awakened my soul to how important it is for us to share the Faith with whomsoever Bahá'u'lláh chooses to guide towards us. At any given moment we could have this most honorable task and it could be our last opportunity.

11

Living Outside the Box

Chris Bishop

I remember the first time I realized that there was something a little different about me. I was four years old and my family and I had just moved into a new apartment. We had ordered cable and subscribed to the Disney Channel. I had eagerly turned on the television set and had begun to watch an old re-run of *The Mickey Mouse Club*. I sat there in envious awe as I watched the kids marching one by one, singing the theme song. My father stepped into the room and asked me to change the station.

'What!' I protested. 'Why? It's Mickey Mouse! I love Mickey Mouse!'

'Because they never allowed black people on that show,' my father replied.

I gazed down at my skin and looked at its light brown tint. I examined my father and his ebony glow. I recalled my beautiful mother and her soft ivory skin. Images of everybody I knew raced through my head: my best friend next door – she was white. My two friends in the apartment next to us – they were black. Suddenly I viewed everybody in my life in a whole new way.

I now knew how to separate people and I knew how other people would separate me. People were no longer just people. They were black, white, Asian, Hispanic and everything in between. Never before had I seen these differences. Is this what Adam and Eve felt like when they realized they were naked? Until this point I had not known about the 'forbidden fruit' called racism. At such a young and tender age, I was subjected to its foul and bitter taste.

I grew up in upstate New York, the haven for people trying to escape the despair of the city. There was a very large Puerto Rican community there. Having light skin and soft, curly hair, I was often taken to be a Puerto Rican. I recall one instance when I was at the house of a friend. His mother was talking to us about racism. The conversation was deep and I was really enjoying it when all of a sudden she began speaking in Spanish! I was not quite sure whether I should tell her that I didn't speak Spanish but she sounded as if she was letting out a great deal of pain and I was scared to interrupt her. So I listened, hoping that what little Spanish I had learned in eighth grade would help me. I soon realized that my Spanish vocabulary was very limited and my friend's mother was not going to say one of the short familiar phrases we learned at school. So I listened to her and I listened and then I listened some more. I listened for 20 minutes, hearing this woman speak with great emotion and intensity. Finally she stopped, and my friend had the chance to tell his mother that I did not speak Spanish. She apologized and gave me a quick summary of what she had said.

Junior high school was sometimes a real test and challenge for me. I moved often during my junior high years and found myself in many different situations. For two years I attended a school where I was one of only three African-Americans. Ignorance was the main problem there. I was often expected to do certain things, like play basketball, dance and listen to rap. I found myself the victim of constant ridicule. One lunchtime one of the 'head bangers' walked up to me and stuck his finger in my hamburger. It was really hard for me to sit there and take it but for some reason I was not interested in fighting. I knew in my heart that there was a better way to fight this terrible pain called racism.

My experience in my last year of junior high, which was at a predominantly Hispanic and African-American school, was very different from that in the predominantly white school. My most vivid memory is of the cafeteria. As I walked in, I immediately noticed that it was segregated along strict racial lines. Everybody sat with their own race. I faced the terrible problem of trying to place myself but there was nowhere for me to go. I ended up sitting by myself for a while until I could find some friends who would accept me. Eventually, I ended up sitting at an integrated table with mainly blacks and Hispanics, one of the few in the cafeteria. Unfortunately, I never sat with whites. It was definitely 'uncool' to be white at my school and I was forced to suppress that side of my identity.

I am the product of a new era. The days of segregation are over. The great American melting pot has formed and people like myself are the main ingredients. In earlier times people like me were called 'accidents' or 'misfits'. This is a new time and there are far too many interracial children for society to deny. But a new question now arises: Where does this new group fit in? In earlier years everything was easily divided into 'black' and 'white'. With interracial kids it is no longer easy. Humans, especially Americans, have a tendency to want to separate everything into categories, to put everything into squares and rectangles. Almost everything we make is in the shape of some kind of square. Everything has to be clear cut and defined, including people. But in this new day, a new view must be taken.

'Abdu'l-Bahá described humanity as a garden:

> Anyone who goes into a rose garden will see various roses, white, pink, yellow, red, all growing together and replete with adornment. Each one accentuates the beauty of the other. Were all of one color, the garden would be monotonous to the eye. If they were all white or yellow or red, the garden would lack variety and attractiveness; but when the colors are varied, white, pink, yellow, red, there will be the greatest beauty. Therefore, I hope that you will be like a rose garden. Although different in colors, yet – praise be to God! – you receive rays from the same sun. From one cloud the rain is poured upon you. You are under the training of one Gardener, and this Gardener is kind to all.[7]

After my experiences in junior high and high school, I decided that it was time for me to leave New York. I decided to attend Maxwell International Bahá'í School in British Columbia, Canada. At the time I was not a Bahá'í but I greatly valued the Bahá'í teaching of unity in diversity. At Maxwell I found myself in a markedly different situation from anything I had ever experienced. My classmates were a very diverse group of Bahá'í youth. The difference between the Bahá'í youth and many other youth is that Bahá'ís know the importance of unity in diversity and they actually strive for it. At Maxwell I learned how to appreciate my background.

The times of separating and classifying are over. It has become way too hard and it can only become harder. By genetic standards I have just as much right to join the Ku Klux Klan as I do the Black Panthers. In the United States we have the $\frac{1}{16}$ rule. If you are $\frac{1}{16}$ of a particular minority then you can classify yourself as that minority. Is this a fair judgment? If my great-grandmother was Native American, does that mean that I know what it truly feels like to be a Native American? I am half black but I feel that it is a mistake for me to call myself definitively black or definitively white. I am half black and half white, so when I am asked to check a box, I enthusiastically choose 'other'.

Recently I was getting a haircut when the hairdresser asked me about my ethnic origin. She wanted to be able to classify me, to put me into a category, a common urge. I told her that I am half African-American and half Caucasian. She told me that I looked Hispanic. I laughed to myself as I realized that I am one of the first of many future generations of 'hybrids' in the Garden of God.

We are trying to maintain our old ways of separation and segregation. As a human race, we have to face the fact that we are no longer little tribes and villages separated by natural barriers. Any one of us can hop on a plane and be on the other side of the globe tomorrow. With the stroke of a key we can write a letter to friends in Australia or China. We can pick up the phone and talk to a friend in Iceland. Our vision must be world embracing – it is futile for us to resist it. Is there anyone out there who can deny the fact that we are all connected? It is time to make adjustments. 'The earth is but one country, and mankind its citizens.'[8]

12

Case in Point

An Interview with Layli Miller-Bashir by Hope Turpin

Layli Miller-Bashir, 25, lived in Vienna, Virginia, at the time of this interview. She had recently established the Tahirih Justice Center, a source of legal action assisting women facing international human rights abuses through the provision of legal aid and social services. Layli became known as a passionate defender of women's rights through her involvement with Fauziya Kassindja, an African who had fled to America to escape the threat of genital mutilation. Layli was able to obtain freedom for the woman, resulting in a historic legal milestone. I was fortunate to have an opportunity to interview Layli in Monteagle, Tennessee. We focused on how Layli views the relationship between women and men and how we can continue to foster partnership. Layli encourages women to speak out more clearly and effectively. She says that without a voice, our goal of reaching equality is unattainable.

Hope: What made you take Fauziya Kassindja's case?

Layli: I took Fauziya's case while I was working as a law clerk in an immigration law firm. The law firm was handling the case and when they asked me to become involved I immediately reacted with excitement. Fauziya's case dealt with issues that were very important to me: the equality of women and men, immigrants' rights and female genital mutilation. Deciding whether or not to take her case was not even an option for me. Of course I would help.

Hope: Did anything surprise you about that case?

Layli: Many things surprised me about Fauziya's case. I think that the thing I found most shocking was how our own country treated her when she came to the United States asking for asylum. She was put in prison, with American convicted felons, for over 17 months. She was shackled, strip-searched, beaten, refused medical care and forced to live in very degrading conditions. I was shocked. I didn't know that we in America – the land of the free – could treat people like this. She had done nothing wrong. She only came here asking for protection, yet this was her reception. The behavior of the immigration judge in her case was also shocking to me. He didn't believe her story of being forced to marry a man twice her age, who already had three other wives, and of being forced to undergo female genital mutilation. The judge yelled at her frequently, was very rude and quite insensitive. I was very surprised that our immigration system treated people who come to this country asking for help with such cruelty.

Hope: What impact did the case have on you?

Layli: Fauziya's case had a significant impact on me personally. It made me more committed than ever to the plight of women who suffer human rights abuses and to the rights of immigrants. It gave me valuable experience in representing refugees and helped to focus my professional aspirations. Fauziya's case also had a significant impact on immigration law in the United States. It established, for the first time, the threat of female genital mutilation as a reason for being a refugee in the United States. Because of Fauziya's case, women who refuse to undergo the tribal ritual can now be protected under United States immigration law.

Hope: You started the Tahirih Justice Center. What was your inspiration?

Layli: After Fauziya's case I began to receive phone calls from women like her who needed help. I realized that there was a real need to offer free legal assistance to women who were being abused and faced human rights violations because most of them couldn't afford a traditional lawyer and couldn't find any help. I started the Tahirih Justice Center to provide assistance to those women.

Hope: What difficulties and successes has this Center experienced?

Layli: The Center has grown so quickly. There are so many women in need of our help and more approach us for representation than we can accept. We really have had many more successes than difficulties. Many well-respected people in the field of refugee law have become involved in the Center. We have been asked to assist with some very exciting projects and have been able to help numerous women receive protection from abuses.

Hope: What stage is the Center at now?

Layli: The Center is fully operational. We have offices in Falls Church, Virginia. We have several interns and are always looking for more. We provide legal services to women facing human rights abuses. We are able to refer our clients to free medical care. We are also developing reports on the condition of women in other countries. The reports help us convince the judges that women are treated badly in their home countries and that they should, therefore, not be forced to return to a place where they will be abused.

Hope: Any discussion of women's rights and equality requires – at the very least – an understanding of the definitions of both of these terms. In your approach to the topic of women and women's rights, how do you define equality?

Layli: I don't know what equality looks like. None of us knows. The idea of equality is limited by our perspective and experiences. The Bahá'í definition of equality, however, is completely different. Its theory is based on the Bahá'í writings. Let me explain: there can be equality through two lines of action. The first pathway of action is through individual transformation, i.e. Who am I? What kind of education did I receive? Examples include the education of women and practical training skills like public speaking, which every woman should master. The second line of action is through justice. Many people underrate the importance of consultation in achieving justice. For example, in historical terms, women have been dominated by force. But if we use consultation within the family, it will act as a catalyst for more productive models of equality, which will result in a more unified group of people. According to 'Abdu'l-Bahá, both the individual and society have roles. The individual is responsible for his or her own transformation, while society's responsibility is to implement justice fully. A legal case provides the perfect example. In a legal case, you have both the individual and society fully absorbed into its dynamics, with each party playing its respective role.

Hope: In what ways would equality – as you have defined it – extend into the realms of politics, business, law, education and religion? What general changes would have to occur for 'equality' to exist in any of those areas?

Layli: Politics is currently a very turbulent area but is also a pivotal area of possible change. A lot of the laws will have to change. The requirements for a witness make it difficult for women to testify, especially in cases of rape or victimization. There is more danger of women being physically and mentally harmed than before, despite police protection of the victim. Judges also have the capacity to be insensitive, which doesn't help solve the problem at all. In the realm of business, women are not fully allowed to have time to go home and be mothers. Sadly, the world of business does not encourage the making of good fathers. A good father would stay at home and spend just as much time with the child as the mother does. Law is based on patriarchy. Therefore, the current system under which we live is not acceptable. I would recommend that all people involved in the law take sensitivity training workshops because to function in a satisfactory law environment, both sexes must be treated equally without hesitation. In education, we need to instill more qualitative openness in our children. We need to stop ostracizing men from the realm of education as well. A change needs to take place in our school curricula, a change which helps our individual children freely understand the concept of equality in an effective way.

Hope: The word 'feminist' has gained a great deal of value-laden baggage from the mass media. Does feminism fit in with your approach to women's rights?

Layli: I personally do like the word feminism, just like anyone who is striving for or working for equality. There is nothing wrong with the term. There is no *one* kind of feminism. There are probably one thousand kinds of feminism, so it is not fair to say that I'm against the use of that term.

Hope: Some have pointed out that equality cannot be attained because men and women simply aren't the same. How would you respond to this assessment?

Layli: I think people should understand that equality doesn't necessarily mean sameness. The term equality is often misunderstood and misrepresented. Equality cannot be attained unless men *help* women achieve the greatness that is theirs. When women advance to the same level as men, men will also advance.

Hope: Religion has played a key role in the lives of those who argue on either side of the women's rights issue. Where does the Bahá'í Faith come into your own interest and activities in this field?

Layli: It is a purely spiritual issue for me. As a spiritual being, my own practices and beliefs do affect my work and my perspective on life in general but I believe that I need to understand my own spirituality in order to establish a relationship between my soul and the work that I do.

Hope: In what way do you see the differences between men and women hindering the attainment of equality? Are there any benefits to be found in the differences?

Layli: We often misunderstand each other. The differences are not hindrances. The differences are good and we complement each other. There are a lot of benefits in these differences. Women in particular have good qualities, even though they think they are weak. A good example is the workplace. When a woman goes to her job, she plays the game men play. Instead of accepting the rules, women need to become part of the environment *and* change the environment – not just acclimatize but also change the rules. For example, women often care more about their feelings, their more intuitive workings, but in the workplace this is seen as a weakness: 'She cares too much.' Women should not get too emotional but by caring more, women can make everyone happy.

Hope: How can women and men, separately and as a group, help speed up the process towards equality? How can they contribute to this goal? Is there any agency they can reach out to for guidance?

Layli: Both women and men have important roles to play. In fact, we cannot have equality without men. Men have to make the equality of women and men their issue. Men need to be a part of attaining equality because until we have equality, men cannot be all they can be. The inequality of men and women is a hindrance to *men*. They need to recognize that. Men need to examine their own behavior, they need to talk about themselves and understand some of their assumptions about women. They need to examine behaviors that are cultural – inherited from the family – and women also need to look at their own behavior because some women do things that are not conducive to equality. For example, when men and women are speaking, women often apologize for their opinions. They need to do things with confidence and be capable, confident and courteous. Sometimes being quiet is easier but if the world is to be all it can be, we need *both* men and women participating. There are lots of organizations but the Bahá'í Office of Women's Affairs is great; it can offer some guidance. It is also responsible for helping the Bahá'í community address the issue of equality.

Hope: Children grow up today seeing a definite lack of equality in school. Math classes favor girls early on but they favor boys once students hit middle school. The arts seem to be reserved for women and sports for men. Is this an example of inequality or simply a recognition of real differences?

Layli: It is important that both men and women have the same opportunities. The problems arise when they are not offered the same opportunities.

Hope: Layli, thank you so much for all of your rewarding insights. You are truly an inspiration for those of us who have a burning passion to see equality change from a much-discussed concept into reality!

Layli: You are very much welcome and thank you for giving me this opportunity! I would like to make one last comment: I want all women to strive with their hearts and souls to fulfill their capacity because the world needs their participation, big time!

13

Stepping from the Sidelines

Amelia Villagómez

It was the first day of school and I was sitting in my theater arts class. Our assignment was to get into pairs, interview our partner and write a report about him or her, which we would then deliver in front of the class. We were to conclude our speeches by giving our opinion of our partner.

After interviewing my partner I sat and pondered. How could I best explain to the class Tony's personality? He seemed like an interesting, intellectual person and I wanted to demonstrate that. The teacher called time and we began presenting. I raised my hand quickly to volunteer. I was excited. I went off on a long description of Tony's interests, hobbies, favorites and his summer adventures. I concluded by telling the class what a great asset he would be to our school and what a great mind he had.

I listened attentively to the other students' speeches and gradually I noticed that my opinion of Tony was drastically different from my peers' opinions of their partners. Most everyone else said that their partner was a 'nice and normal' teenager.

Nice and normal? What is 'normal'? Does it mean that you fit in with the rest of society and don't have any qualities that distinguish you? Does it mean that you meet society's expectations without trying to generate your own expectations for yourself? Does it mean that you're not different, thus you're well-liked?

Throughout my life, I've wanted to make myself known for who I am and what I stand for. In fifth grade I'd wear a button to school every day with a message on it, like 'Racism: Just Undo It' or 'Enough Tears, Stop the Killing' or 'Unity in Diversity'. That was my fool-proof plan for people to notice me and discover my personality.

I wondered why no one else was committed to such a hobby. As I matured, I learned that most everyone wanted to be 'normal' and not attract attention to their views. I'd sit in home room and watch girls apply blusher, mascara and lipstick. They'd laugh and giggle and act like 'normal' teenage girls. They did not want to attract attention to themselves except through their beauty. They would sit in class but would never share their opinions on a life-threatening issue or raise a hand to answer a math problem. They simply sat there with confused looks and pretended that the subject didn't matter.

I knew many of the 'normal' people. They tried to fit in by acting like everyone else and by suppressing their own uniqueness. They were wonderful, bright, talented – and they really did care about current events. So why didn't they show it? Would this make them veer from the 'normal' standard? What had made them want to be 'normal'? Were they scared of being different? Was it uncool to be yourself?

I would soon learn. At recess there were numerous activities to fill the time. There was basketball, soccer and football. I noticed, however, that most of the girls stood in groups talking. I loved sports, so I decided to play basketball during recess despite the unspoken pressure from the 'normal' girls to conform.

When I was small, we played basketball in our backyard. My father used to throw me on his shoulder so I could make slam dunks, and to help me develop my independence, a shorter hoop was made just for me. My brother and sister would play 'Cat or Dog' with me, and although I'd frequently lose, a love for dribbling and shooting was implanted in my spirit.

I approached the court with a dozen boys staring at me from the sidelines. I didn't understand exactly why. I asked, 'Can I play?' They started laughing. Frankly, I didn't see the problem. Then the guys all informed me that basketball was a man's game.

I still didn't understand why I couldn't play. Sports aren't dependent on gender but rather on skill. Why should I be turned away from a game I love because of something I have no control over? Was playing basketball not 'normal' for women, yet 'normal' for men? I asked for a chance. They thought about it and decided it would be terrible to pass up a good laugh. So they gave me permission to enter the game.

I was quick and good on defense, so I concentrated on blocking. I found the best player and blocked him. When he got the ball, I swept my hands in front of it and quickly got a steal.

Suddenly, everyone became quiet. They were shocked. The dozen boys on the sidelines were in awe. I could see the gaping mouths on each of their faces. When they recovered, they started shouting, 'You got taken up by a girl!'

The others looked at me in shock, as if they were wondering how a girl could out-do a guy. I took the ball and shot from the three point line. Swoosh, I made it! They stood there, in silent astonishment, jaws hanging open.

Still, I hadn't earned my equality. In spite of my skill, there was something unchangeable running against me: my gender. Was this how sexism overtakes justice? I'd steal the ball and pass it to one of my team mates to give him a chance to share the spotlight, yet no one ever returned the favor and passed the ball back to me. Was I really on their team or were they all against me? They might have realized my skill but they still wouldn't accept it.

I looked out past the sidelines to the groups of girls talking. In a way, I was sad that I couldn't be with them. I felt as though we were in totally separate worlds. Yet, in another way, I felt triumphant, almost joyful. The girls in groups may not have understood the basketball-playing boys, yet both the girls and boys were forced to ask themselves the question: what exactly is the station of women? Are women just walking models of outer perfection? Is that all a woman can attain – outer perfection? Is that the goal of a woman – to be a beautiful statue? Isn't there something for women other than being 'normal'? Perhaps we should change our standards of normality so that pursuing our own goals becomes normal.

Women have wonderful characteristics. We should be proud of our femininity. Femininity is being considerate, kind and loving – qualities which God gave us. We must transform a world obsessed with physical dominance into a world that radiates virtues. 'Abdu'l-Bahá said:

> The world in the past has been ruled by force, and
> man has dominated over woman by reason of his

more forceful and aggressive qualities both of body and mind. But the balance is already shifting; force is losing its dominance, and mental alertness, intuition, and the spiritual qualities of love and service, in which woman is strong, are gaining ascendancy.[9]

This is our true goal.

Why do women starve themselves? Why are they tormented by their weight and appearance? What they look like is only a small part of who they are. As women we must love ourselves. We must not judge our worth by our reflection in a mirror because a mirror can't reflect true beauty. We must aim for a higher beauty. In life there are two beauties: one we can control, the inner and true beauty, and the other which we must not allow to control us, the outer beauty. Our inner beauty is our character. We must be detached from our outer being and *arise*. We must aim higher. We do not, however, have to aim for all of men's goals, for we are equal but different. We have heard this statement so many times, yet what does it mean? Why did God make us different, while at the same time requiring us to reach a state of equality? Men and women have different qualities which make them superior in their own ways. I believe women have a natural sense of love and gentleness while men have the ability to lead and dominate with both physical and emotional force and ambition. Would it be sensible for women to strive for the qualities of men?

Living in a society obsessed with materialism, women are constantly battling to develop themselves internally rather than just externally. Sometimes it may seem like banging our heads against a wall. Every time we turn on the television or look on the front cover of a magazine, we see examples of outward perfection. We must fight against the overbearing emphasis on outer beauty. We must seek justice within ourselves and throughout society. We must educate ourselves.

It is my family, and especially my sister Martha, who has given me the courage to demand equality even when I doubt my skills. My sister is a very special person, probably not much different from you and me. It's the little things she does every day that give me courage, not just one big thing. She considers me her 'project'! Every day when

I come home from school, she asks me how I'm doing and how my day went. When I told her about the basketball games, she told me to rest assured that things would be all right. If you asked me what advice she gave me, I couldn't tell you exactly what it was, I just remember the spirit it was given in and the message it sent to my heart: 'Stick in there.' She encourages me by doing little things, like giving me a kiss every other hour and telling me that I have a mission, that I truly am someone special. When I wonder if someone cares about me or if someone supports me, I know that I am surely loved.

Martha wasn't on the basketball court cheering me on, or even on the sidelines, but she was the source of my inspiration. To be a hero and change someone's life, you don't have to have a special talent or gift; you just have to open your heart and send messages of support and love.

As women, we are important. It is not the men alone who can change the world. We must be strong, yet loving. We must show the world what it can mean to be feminine. We must understand our station in the world. If we continue to be 'normal' and just settle for what is expected of us without allowing our potential to be seen, how will we change the world? We mustn't remain 'normal' and allow the world to decay. We must *arise*. Together with men, we will surely destroy the foundations of war and build a world with the attributes of love and unity – a world of balance.

14

Call to Excellence

Meghan Morris

The Bahá'í International Community: United Nations Office. The name held importance and sounded imposing, exciting. When I found out that I would become an intern in that office, I had visions dancing in my head for weeks. I imagined the powerful diplomats I might meet, the decisions I would witness, the anticipation I would feel every day of my internship, the knowledge that in some way I could make a contribution to this institution – one that represents the stepping stone of this civilization to the precipice of a new world order.

I had held this dream since I was ten years old. I had gone to New York City with my father and as part of our tourist ventures we took the usual tour of the United Nations buildings. As corny as it may sound, I found myself in awe of the tour guide. Her presence amazed me. She knew the history, she led us through council chambers, she explained the background of the artwork but more than this – she had a reason to come to the UN every day. I wanted that sense of purpose. In my ten-year-old mind I started brainstorming the possibilities. I thought maybe I could work in the UN gift store someday. From the time I understood what an internship was, I knew I wanted one at the UN.

I held onto my dream for 11 years and finally found it realized in a far different capacity than I had ever anticipated. The dreams I carried with me to the first day of my internship at the BIC's United Nations Office seem arrogant and naive when I think back. The experience did not fail to supply me with inspiration but it was a more subtle and personal transformation than my imagination ever could have conjured up.

I went to New York City as one of 28 students in the National Collegiate Honors Council Semester. The council offers a semester in a city of interest somewhere in the world each year. The theme changes depending on the location. The theme of the semester had lured me more than New York City itself – Globalization and Communication. The 28 of us represented different colleges and universities throughout the country. We each brought our own views of globalization to our internship agencies and organizations and we each left changed in some way. Some people worked at television stations like NBC or CBS; some worked in marketing firms; several worked for museums; others worked for cutting-edge magazines. Two worked for a non-profit service provider for youth, while one student worked as the private intern for a celebrity singer. The diversity of our internship sites mirrored the diversity of the group itself.

The 28 of us immediately began our adjustment to life in the city: maneuvering the subways, keeping pace with the constantly moving crowds that inhabit New York's sidewalks, seeking the cheapest restaurants and sleeping through the night without allowing the sounds of sirens to awaken us.

As we encountered obstacles in this process, I knew I had a strength in my internship that few had – the feeling that I had a second family in my co-workers. This connection began during the first morning of my internship and grew stronger as time went on.

That first morning, I rode the Four train by myself and got off at Grand Central Station. I walked down to the United Nations Plaza, dodging hurried business people and trying to keep their pace. I developed the attitude that if I could walk as fast as or even faster than these rushed New Yorkers, then no one would bother me. It seemed to work. I never got mugged or even threatened, though divine protection may account for this more than my attitude.

On that first full day of my internship, though, I still lacked confidence as I made my way down the busy streets and by the time I made it to the office, I had entered a state of shock. I walked in overwhelmed, out of breath and feeling slightly lost, even though I knew my physical location. I had to use all my energy to hold back tears of frustration. I had come to New York after spending a year doing volunteer service in rural Oklahoma, in a little town where everyone greeted one another on the street. I couldn't walk down the street there without seeing at least four or five people I knew. It took only five minutes to cross that small town. Though I came from a decent-sized city, I felt New York City's size more profoundly because of the year spent in Oklahoma.

Dorothy Longo, my supervisor, saw my confusion and soothed my nerves. She told me to take it easy. 'We want you to enjoy your time here,' she told me as she handed me a prayer book and a Kleenex and allowed me to recover from the pains of my culture shock. 'Remember, we are your family while you are here.'

I recovered, anxious for my orientation. My first day filled me with awe as I witnessed the flow of faxes back and forth to the Bahá'í World Centre in Haifa, Israel, and to National Spiritual Assemblies all over the world. I was amazed by the communication that went through the office, at all of the information at our fingertips. But most astounding was the level of interpersonal communication and the openness of all who worked at the BIC.

In other offices that I had worked in, people always complained that communication could be better. They wanted to know more about what others were working on and have more information about projects that pertained to them. I never heard these complaints at the BIC. If someone had a problem or a question, consultation immediately took place. Much of the office's strength comes from the unique ability to consult and to overcome challenges in a unified manner, instead of having the skirmishes and status competitions that often impede organizations. I knew I would see the principles of the Bahá'í Faith manifested in daily actions at the BIC but I couldn't know how my own understanding and hope for humanity would strengthen as I witnessed and became a part of this incredible group of people.

Within the first two weeks of my internship, the need arose for me to assist in a project that would become one of the first of its kind for the office and for the Bahá'í world. I helped with the binding and mailing of a document on Human Rights Education which will serve as a reference manual for national communities. Because of the collaboration among staff members in the implementation of this project, I had the chance to see firsthand the respect and level of communication within the BIC's United Nations Office.

I worked primarily under two supervisors, who over time became like my big brother and sister in the office – Ellen and John. Ellen was the Aide to Stephen Karnik, the Chief Administrative Officer (CAO) and John was the Aide to Lawrence Arturo, Director of the Office of the Environment. I soon learned that these titles helped in understanding one's greater task but they by no means defined someone's identity or the respect they were given. Ellen and John were the people who structured my day. They assigned the order of my tasks – telling me to take the tabs off binders or to collate 110 copies of sections A and B. Could I have them ready by the end of the day? They checked on my progress throughout, taking time away from the editing they did downstairs to help me when they could.

John and Ellen explained that they had worked together for six or more years. They knew one another's thoughts, ideas and potential struggles and this made them stronger as a team. They became an example to me of the manifestation of the true equality of men and women. If I had a question or if something went wrong and I asked John, and he couldn't answer immediately, he always said Ellen would know. He told me, 'We consult about everything.' It was true. I saw how they would come up with a better result after careful consultation – John would think of something Ellen hadn't; Ellen would have a new idea or they would come up with something between the two of them. I never saw a hierarchy: I saw equality and a unity that ran throughout the entire office.

As people got accustomed to my presence, I soon found myself a part of that unity. Others in the office would drop by the room where I did most of my collating and share stories. Lawrence, the Director of the Office of the Environment, often wandered in to ask how I was and what I was thinking about and somehow ended up sharing stories about his time as a Peace Corps volunteer in Mauritania. He would help me with whatever task I had in front of me and thank me for helping him take a break from his desk. He was never condescending to me; he never created a hierarchy between us.

I observed more of this in the male-female dynamics of the office. Power existed not as something that came from an individual ego but as something written in the Bahá'í writings and as something a unified group could create in service to humanity. Responsibility replaced power, as it should.

As we struggled to meet deadlines on the publication, I found Steve, the CAO, huddled around the table with the rest of us, stacking cardboard boxes and mulling through address labels. At the time, I never considered it odd that Steve should help. Everyone who had time came to lend a hand. But as I look back, I realize that many would consider this sort of work to be beneath them. In the BIC, 'beneath' didn't exist in its usual context.

Seeing the efficiency created by this paradigm shift allowed me to glimpse the future. I have a deeper longing for humanity's unity, for honesty and justice to prevail, for people of all ethnic backgrounds to see themselves as spiritual beings and for the equality of men and women to be realized. I have seen the amount of good accomplished in this microcosm where individuals understood these principles and fused them: work as worship.

I learned the most from two distinct parts of each day: the beginning and the middle. Each day work began by gathering at nine o'clock for prayers. Though attendance was not mandatory, I practically sprinted from the subway station on days I was running late in order not to miss prayers. I cherished the time when I could gather with these souls, raise my voice alongside theirs and feel the unity they had. I felt that perhaps my prayers could contribute equally with my service, that if I could raise up my voice in prayer for unity or protection for humanity, then in some small, indirect way, maybe I could assist in the tasks that others faced each day.

The other ritual I looked forward to, for different reasons, was lunch, which was a time of unity and sharing, literally and figuratively. At first I wondered about all these foods in the middle of the table, little yellow post-it notes stuck on them with the letters 'P.D.' Someone explained that this was office slang for 'Public Domain', which meant that whatever was in the middle was free for the taking. People were incredibly generous and I never left the kitchen hungry. Someone brought an extra cake that didn't get eaten at their home or leftovers from a weekend dinner party. Several women in the office made it a daily custom to have a potluck with one another – each contributing something they knew the other liked.

In the kitchen people also shared their stories and those of their families. They shared memories of trips in Australia, of grandmothers in Georgia, of Bahá'ís in Zimbabwe, and told me stories about their children and grandchildren. I would sometimes reciprocate the sharing and tell a story from my own past. As I talked, others would enter, and as they unwrapped their lunch bags or waited to use the microwave, they would listen sincerely, as eager to know more about me as I was about them. I believe this casual sharing reinforced the sense of family. It made this ideal become a reality and it demonstrated that the office had a true love and unity that bound it, not something superficial that vanished as office doors were closed. When individuals felt tested or had an illness in their family, they knew that people in the office would pray for them, support them, comfort them.

Today, the office place has become a battleground for many men and women – a field of competition where every individual must climb some illusory ladder and step on souls that might hinder their way. Equality is measured by paychecks and rank. We have surrendered honesty and kindness. How can we truly know work as worship if we abandon our moral principles?

The sooner we change the way we communicate in our workplaces, the sooner we will see the standards change. The UN looks to the Bahá'ís as an example of excellence – in the quality of their documents, the speed of their responses to questions and their presence and contributions in committee meetings. I saw this excellence firsthand. I know that the quality of their work comes from careful consultation, from each individual's contribution along the way and from a unity that defines each conversation.

My experience at the BIC has forever changed my standards for a place of work. I want to give respect, consult openly and remedy communication problems instead of allowing them to cause disunity. I want to encompass the excellence that the UN has found in the Bahá'ís. I have a new responsibility. I know the BIC represents a few unique working situations that exist in the world as we know it today but the sooner that we begin to change the way that we communicate in our workplaces, the sooner we will see the standards change.

15

River Seed

An Interview with River Brandon by Ojan Vafá'í

River Brandon, chief designer of *One* magazine and partner in Unit.E – a design business he runs with his wife Heather – is a new father. He and Heather moved to western Massachusetts from southern Maine so River could start a job at an advertising agency. I asked River what it's like to be a new dad along with all the other changes in his life and what new challenges he is facing.

Ojan: You recently had your first child – a daughter. How has this affected your life?

River: It's been profound. There was a whole process that led up to the birth of our child: Heather and I deciding to have a child; considering how our lives would change and what we needed to do to be ready; thinking what it means to provide a good, loving family and home for a new child. I think the fundamental thing was striving as much as we could to work on our marriage and relationship in essential ways, being unified, being able to communicate effectively, knowing our priorities and putting our faith in God at the center of our marriage – all of this so our child would have a stable reality and we would have somewhere to draw the energy and love required to raise a new person in this world.

That was a lot of work and then the whole pregnancy process made everything more intense and we focused more on what it meant to us to have a child and how it would affect our daily lives. We realized that it would be unpredictable in a lot of ways. The best way to handle unpredictability is to have a strong foundation. We worked on talking to each other about how we were feeling and what we were going through. Obviously, Heather, being pregnant, went through tons of changes, physically and emotionally, so it was a lot of work for me to try to understand what that was like

60

for her and much of that was just listening and asking questions. Then Council, our daughter, was born and for the past month there's been a lot of adjusting and a continuation of the efforts to communicate and be clear with each other about what we feel our personal needs are, priorities and things we have to get done. We spend a lot of time just focusing on the child, learning what she has to teach us and what it means to be responsible for her and educate her.

Ojan: You talked about unpredictability and having a strong foundation. In a Bahá'í marriage and family, one of the key aspects to this foundation is the equality of women and men. How do you feel this expresses itself in both your marriage and in your new role as a father?

River: I think the most important thing is to have unity. I definitely think if you have unity and you can get to a point of practicing equality in a relationship, then it's twice as strong because you don't have the power focused on one individual – it gets shared. Any time you have a system – and I think this holds true for the natural world around us, machines, human groups of people, any system we look at – the more power is distributed and the stresses spread out across the system, the more stable the system is in the long run. The whole thing is going to last as well as the individual parts last. In a marriage, the more things can be shared – decision-making, responsibilities or the needs of the relationship – the stronger the foundation. If you try to be flexible without the factor of unity, then things get torn apart. You need strong pieces and really good glue for the whole thing to stick together. You've asked how the equality of women and men has been manifested in our relationship. In my experience it is a practice. It's something I do from moment to moment, as opposed to something I get to have.

Ojan: It's something that develops over time, you mean?

River: Yeah, it develops and grows over time but it's also a goal that is never achieved because it's a practice. Like if you're a musician, you play music. That's what being a musician is: it's a practice, not a thing. Equality in a relationship, or in any group of people, has to be a practice everybody participates in and everybody tries to play their part to move things in a good direction. So you take individual responsibility for the greater reality, the greater good. For me, that comes down in practical terms to communication as one of the most fundamental things I can do in that practice. When you're dealing with two or three human beings in a family, the only way you have to be unified and participate in the work of equality is by communicating, by making sure that you understand what's going on with the other person, where they're coming from and that they understand you and that you try to move in a direction together. It doesn't happen unless you talk. Communication skills are something I work on every day. I think it's hard being a man because we aren't educated to be the communicators we really need to be to have healthy relationships and stable families. This may just be part of being male but, at least historically, we don't have the same sort of style of communicating that women do, so there's a lot of work to do to bridge that gap.

Ojan: Can you expand on that a bit? What do you mean by different styles of communication?

River: One thing is quantity – women tend to communicate more of the details of life. There's a lot of emotional meaning in the details of life and, in my experience, women talk about these and communicate with each other more than men do. I've read something which has rung true in my experience as well: that there is a hierarchical nature to male communications while there is more equality in female communications. I'm referring to men talking to men and women talking to women. I think the male style is to try to establish dominance or a position in the hierarchy in terms of what we say, what we talk about or express. So I think men are frequently, if not always, vying for the dominant position in a conversation – one-upmanship.

For example, if two men are talking about something as sweet and wonderful as their children, it can often turn into a discussion about the accomplishments of their children. Women tend to look for connections on a more equal level and create a bond that goes both ways, one that's about a sharing of experience and information and doesn't necessarily translate into status. For example, if they're talking about their children, they might share stories about their children that establish something common for both of them – maybe an illness that both of their children have had or an experience in school or whatever. So connectivity is the goal there, whereas for men it's to figure out who's going to be the alpha male.

These are old-fashioned patterns. The world is in such an interesting state of flux right now. These things are changing and being redefined. We have the job of changing all this so there's a much better balance in terms of how men and women communicate and co-exist.

When a man is talking to a woman about something – whether it's family or business – often the man is looking to establish dominance and falls into that competitive role. The woman generally won't try to pick up the ball and play that game because she's looking for a sympathetic connection. Often women come out of those situations feeling hurt, frustrated or misunderstood and men can be pretty insensitive to that.

Ojan: You segued from family life into society in general. How do you think family life relates to society as a whole?

River: Well, family life is the primary place we learn this stuff – whether it's good or bad. It's our foundation for how we behave and deal with the greater society. Within my family, growing up, I watched my parents and the way they communicated. They definitely had a lot of these kinds of struggles and really made an effort towards equality. I watched them fall short much of the time. But I also feel that I gained a great deal from having a father and a mother who were both aware of the sort of dynamic that can take place. They worked hard to break the patterns that they could easily have fallen into and they taught their kids how to do it better.

I have to say that my dad tends to have some feminine qualities that give him a little more balance and vice-versa – my mother has a some masculine qualities that allow her to have that balance too. She's had some success in dealing with the male-dominated professional world but at the same time she's found it very frustrating because it's dominated by the male style. She's able to see that and sort out what's happening with it and tries to counteract it by doing positive things. I think I've benefited a great deal from watching that experience and listening to her talk about it.

I've come to understand things that don't often get talked about in family settings – the struggles of being a woman in a male-dominated reality or my father's struggle with other men, his peers, trying to figure out where he falls in the hierarchy, what his status is – answering questions like, 'What do you do for a living?' and having to explain his career when he was a homemaker and focused on raising his kids for many years. That doesn't hold a lot of status in the male world, so that's been difficult for him, knowing that it's important that he be a father and a husband and that it's worthy for him to focus on that, yet at the same time realizing that the world doesn't give him a lot of recognition for doing it – it's not highly valued.

I feel like I can identify a lot more with my dad now that I'm married – and now that I have a child, too, because these relationships are so important and they're so amazing. They teach you things that you really can't imagine or think about until you're in it and doing it. I can understand the stresses of the expectations from the outside, or at least what I feel are expectations – that I find a job where I get a lot of recognition for being an expert and get paid well and accumulate the necessary material things and bring home good paychecks for my family. I'm willing to sacrifice some of those things in order to have a more unified family experience, to be able to spend more time with my daughter and experience the process of being in a family. But it's hard to do. Sometimes I wish I could have a job where I could talk to someone and they'd go, 'wow, you do THAT? You work for THEM? You get paid HOW much?' But at the same time, I know that's fleeting, an illusion in a lot of ways.

Ojan: Earlier you mentioned God as a third party in your marriage and you also mentioned unity as the foundation of your marriage. How do you think those two relate?

River: It's through my belief in God and the Bahá'í writings that I've learned about the fundamental importance of unity. I've learned some of the most important tools for achieving unity and maintaining it. That's a crucial part of the relationship – God is our educator and without God's education, we're ignorant and therefore we're unable to progress and achieve things that are important. God gives us the tools and the skills – the training – to do things like try to have equality of the sexes and unity of the races. So in a very personal way, I try to use these as my guide-posts and as my tools in this journey.

At the same time, I think there has to be a unifying force within a relationship. Again I want to emphasize the reality as a process. Unity isn't something we can put in the middle of the living room and the family can be happy and feel good all the time. It's a work in progress, it's a dance that we keep doing together. In order to do that dance, you have to be hearing the same music. Every family, and in general, every group of people that wants to be unified, needs to have a focal point of unity. For example, if you're working for a large corporation, your focal point may be producing a great product or making a profit. You can achieve unity by focusing on that and doing the dance together around that rhythm. But those are temporary things, those are things of this material world that inevitably pass. In my experience, to have a lasting unity and a truly solid foundation, you need a permanent point of unity, one that's going to last forever. And I believe the only thing that lasts forever is God. So I think spirituality and religious faith are the things that, in the long run, truly allow people to maintain strong relationships and healthy families.

My parents have said that if they hadn't shared their belief in Bahá'u'lláh and in God, they probably wouldn't be married at this point because the stresses of the world are really intense. If we don't believe in something greater, then it's easy to understand why more than half the marriages in our country end in divorce. If marriage is a thing of this life, this world, and if it's supposed to be a convenience, well, then, it's pretty darn inconvenient a lot of the time! So there are a lot of great excuses for either not getting married or for getting married and then getting divorced. But if the belief that there's an eternal spiritual reality is shared, then that's a lot greater than any of the difficulties that you come up against in this world.

Ojan: So you feel we'll be able to achieve the equality of women and men by having God as the focal point?

River: Yeah, definitely. If we look back at history, the things that have allowed civilizations to grow and succeed over time have been a fundamental core of shared values. At least in my limited knowledge of history, in the greatest civilizations, those values have been religious morals and teachings. If we look at the fundamentals, at the basis of our American society and democracy, these come from Judeo-Christian religious teachings. Without them, we wouldn't have most of the values we think of as American. Once again we have to have that common rhythm, something that we all put at the center. I think the only thing that can be is God.

Ojan: How do you feel this can be put into effect in society so that people actually believe this and not just see it from a distance?

River: As a Bahá'í, one of my responsibilities is to teach other people who want to know about the Bahá'í Faith. That's the best I can do in terms of getting this stuff out there. My job is to be the conduit for that information to pass through and the rest is really up to God – touching people's hearts and transforming their lives or revealing to them His truth. I don't know if this gets at what you're trying to ask but my job is to clear myself out as best I can to let that stuff come through. And that just happens on an individual level. People of other religions often feel the same way and understand similar things – God is the motivating force here, the source of energy and we just have to be the best circuits we can be to deliver the juice. And that only happens when we choose to do it and make the effort – those connections made from one person to another. It feels like it's going slowly, on a small scale all the time, because it's a personal thing. Once you start building a mass of individuals who share a unity of vision and purpose, that can become a very powerful force. I think it's a very human characteristic – if we see other people doing something and it's working, then we're moved by that and we want to learn what they're doing and emulate that behavior.

Ojan: As you said, there is a traditional difference between women and men's ways of interacting. How do you think this applies to what men can do versus what women can do in order to strive towards this goal of equality?

River: I think men need to watch and listen carefully to women and understand the ways in which they communicate and handle things in life because there's tons men can learn from them. If we can understand those things and find those abilities within ourselves – because I really believe the potential is there – then we can become more balanced ourselves. That makes room for women to find the balance for themselves and part of that is developing some of their masculine qualities. Men have dominated human society and culture for so long now that it falls upon us to make room for this process to happen. I mean, the process is going to happen because God wants it to but I believe that men have the power to hold it off and to cause some major wrinkles in the whole fabric if we resist strongly and persist in our arrogance. It's hard because it's so passive, a yielding thing. We have to listen to women and encourage and support them. It's a new path. If you're part of that half of the human race that's been disempowered for so long, you don't have a whole lot of confidence to tread the new path. Men really have to be supporters and encouragers and helpmates. We've got to make sure that women are able to go where they need to go. According to the Bahá'í teachings, women have a leadership role in the transformation of the world, achieving world peace and the unity of humanity. Men have to be there to support that process and to follow the lead.

16

Standing in the Doorway of Both Worlds

An Interview with Joy Turpin by Hope Turpin

Joy Turpin, my 20-year-old sister, was a third-year student at the University of Tennessee in Knoxville at the time of this interview. Like myself, Joy has been profoundly hearing-impaired since birth. As well as being my sister, Joy is also my best friend. Our closeness as two young hearing-impaired women helped make this interview a wonderfully enriching experience.

Hope: How do you define language?

Joy: Language is not only something spoken out of the mouth, it is also body gestures, including sign language and other simple visual cues that we give out every day as a method of communication. Because of technology we are now able to open vast worlds and networks of human communication. Language can take the form of something small such as a pat on the back or something larger, like a fax out of the White House. Language has many definitions. Cultures give language different levels of importance, which makes a single definition complex. Language is perceived through the diverse eyes and ears of humankind. A culture is affected by the diversity of its language. This is why the idea of forming a universal language is so appealing.

Hope: Did your perspective on language in general change after you learned sign language? What kind of sign language are you most comfortable with?

Joy: Yes. I'm most comfortable with using total communication/SEE. Total communication is defined as a method of using *both* sign language and lip reading. I also employ spoken English on an everyday basis, after having attended years and years of speech therapy and auditory training sessions at a younger age. My perspective on language changed after learning sign language at the age of 13. I can now look at myself and say that I'm standing in the doorway of *both* worlds: the hearing and deaf worlds. It is a true gift, the ability to communicate with both groups of people in a harmonious arrangement. However, there have been some not-so-harmonious situations where I have had to deal with criticism from both sides. I'm pretty sure that happens to everyone, handicapped or not. It's just interesting how they take language as a factor by which an individual can be judged.

Hope: As a deaf individual, do you consider yourself bilingual?

Joy: Yes and proudly so. With my Latin studies in high school, I could even call myself trilingual!

Hope: Do you think everyone, including all hearing individuals, should learn sign language in order for the deaf community to thrive? Should it be mandatory?

Joy: I strongly believe that everyone should know the basics of sign language such as the alphabet or even simple everyday words so that we can easily communicate with the deaf without having to rely on an interpreter.

Hope: How does your use of sign language affect the way you see language and communication in general?

Joy: I think of language as something beautiful but sometimes people take it for granted because they do not realize how far we've progressed as a handicapped segment of our population. It is also a part of our culture and many overlook that fact. Luckily, that seems to be changing with the increased awareness of the unique characteristics that make up our deaf culture.

Hope: Do you feel like you lose or gain anything because of the way you communicate?

Joy: GAIN!!! I have been rewarded with access to a beautiful world with beautiful people with beautiful concepts with beautiful hand gestures. It is different, by far, when compared to how everyone else communicates on an everyday basis, yes, but since I see beauty in being unique, I see the way I communicate as a big diamond in the rough.

17

The Gypsies and Me

Mojan Sami

I have always loved summer, not for the sun, the sand and the surf but for the changes and new experiences. Three years ago I spent my summer backpacking through six western European countries. I met hundreds of people from all over the world, including American backpackers like myself. I had read my European traveler's guide beforehand to prepare myself for the trip. I studied currency exchanges, what to eat, where to sleep, what to do, who to talk to. I even studied the historical backgrounds of various European cities. My only barrier now was language.

I spent three weeks of my voyage in Catalonia, a Spanish province striving for sovereignty. Spain was difficult for me because I only knew one Spanish word, *hola*. But only a few footsteps into the country and I was in love. Never had I seen a country so full of energy and life. From morning until night music echoed through the streets and La Rambla was occupied by people, young and old, dancing to the same beat. I wanted to suck in every last detail. I wanted to remember every person, every moment. I wanted to feel a rush of culture and freedom – and I did.

For a couple of nights I stayed in a youth hostel in Barcelona that had no running water. During the days I explored the streets and shops. One morning, as I was wandering aimlessly through the downtown area (let's face it, I was lost), I came across a sign that said 'Centro Bahá'í de Barcelona'. I couldn't believe that I had stumbled across a Bahá'í Center on the other side of the world. I stepped up to the door without hesitation.

Inside I met a group of Bahá'í youth from various parts of Spain. They were preparing for the European Bahá'í Youth Conference, which would be attended by youth from all over western Europe. They welcomed me and included me to the fullest extent, even though

I didn't speak their language. A young man named Omid, who had studied in the United States for a year, became my translator. He blushed when a young girl asked him to tell me that I had 'romantic eyes' – so *romanticos ojos* became my first Spanish phrase.

The youth in the room were so warm and embracing. They constantly watched me to see what the 'American' would do. They begged me to accompany them on a service project to the small town of Gerona. I didn't know much about the project but that evening I hopped on a train with three Spanish youth: Mariona, Shoghi and Javier.

I really had no idea what we were doing or where we were going. The three of them didn't speak English and did nothing more but smile at me throughout the entire train ride. I doubted my decision to go because I felt so awkward and out of place. But I knew this trip would be special. I knew.

In Gerona, we were greeted by a happy group of Bahá'ís who eagerly took us into their homes. They were surprised that I had joined the group, as I spoke no Spanish, but they were proud to have an international group and glad to have me. They showed us to our bedroom, where the sheets and pillows were laid out for us. We were honored to be treated so kindly. That evening, as we each crawled into our beds, Mariona whispered to me in a nervous, embarrassed tone, 'Good night.' I smiled as she turned off the light.

We woke up bright and early the next morning and every morning after that. I sat quietly at the breakfast table while everyone else chatted and laughed. Every so often I'd notice them notice me – and I think they felt guilty for not being able to converse with me freely. I still listened to their conversations and tried to pick out words and phrases, hoping that maybe I'd learn something. It wasn't until about two days later that I discovered that Shoghi and Mariona had taken high school English and were just embarrassed to use it with a 'real' American.

Our days went by quickly. Every morning we'd take the bus to a *gitano* community. The *gitanos* are the gypsies, victims of prejudice throughout Europe. But some cities, including Gerona, reserve a sector of land to protect the *gitanos* and provide them with rooms in large apartment complexes.

When we arrived, we'd shake the gypsies' hands and one of my companions would explain I was from 'Estados-Unidos'. The gypsies' eyes would widen and mouths would gape. I understood from their exclamations in Spanish that they had never met an American before.

The gypsies were very friendly but none spoke English. Their quality of living was of a very low standard and their cleaning habits poor. Most of them didn't work because the most important job was to take care of their families. Their community was so unified. I couldn't believe the extent to which a *gitano* would go to help another in need. Their hearts were pure, their souls tantalized me. I was frustrated that I couldn't communicate with them but, slowly, we found a way. Music. All the gypsies I met loved music. It was a way for them to pass the time, remain happy and, most of all, remain unified.

We gathered around a small fire as the *gitanos* sang through the night. An elderly woman asked me to sing a song in English and I laughed in shock and embarrassment as she persisted. I shyly sang a song I had written, and as a young man got the hang of the tune, he accompanied me with his guitar. They made me sing it again and again throughout the night and each time our audience grew. People came and peeked into our circle, wondering what was going on. And I could hear whispers from men to women to children: 'Estados-Unidos. Estados-Unidos.'

I had a difficult time understanding the *gitanos* and at first it was hard to enjoy the time I spent with them. I explained to them that I didn't speak Spanish or Catalonian but they continued to talk to me, regardless. I didn't understand why, in the midst of a modern culture, there was this primitive, uneducated lifestyle. I didn't understand why the *gitanos* had been ostracized by their native countrymen or why they were looked upon as dirty and gruesome. In the old days peasants had more worth than the *gitanos*. But they were so pure. They sat around campfires and told stories and sang through the moonlight. They were happy to have each other.

We returned every day. By the end of the week, we were all sobbing in each other's arms, afraid to let each other go. For eight days I had been with a group of people that I didn't understand. We lived in two separate worlds. Their culture and traditions were so drastically different from mine. My culture is at a point where people talk about issues such as drug abuse, youth violence and teenage pregnancy but the gypsies wouldn't dare jinx the day by bringing up these subjects.

A woman pulled me aside on my last day with the community. She told me about her daughter's hardships in an abusive marriage and the translator didn't have to convey her sadness to me. I saw it in her face. She grabbed my hand and took me to a room in one of the apartment complexes. We climbed stairs – it seemed like a hundred of them – until we arrived in the dark, musty room. There were flies everywhere. I flailed my hand in the sticky air to keep them away but the woman did nothing. The flies sat on her face, her hands, her neck and she still remained motionless.

In the center of the room was a young girl, not much older than me, lying on an old sofa. She had bruises on her arms and legs and I tried hard to pretend they weren't there. She turned and said something to her mother, who walked over to her and kissed her face. Her mother whispered in her ear and all I understood was 'Estados-Unidos'.

When the young girl stood up and her sweater fell to her sides, I noticed that she was carrying an unborn child. It was unbelievable, almost surreal, to be there. The woman wasted no time. She immediately turned to me and asked me to sing for her daughter. I didn't know what to sing. I wasn't embarrassed this time, I was scared. I was scared that I was there for no reason at all. Maybe the girl didn't care. I felt I had to do something meaningful for her and I wasn't sure if I could.

The girl smiled and said, *'En ingles?'* She made herself comfortable on the sofa as her eyes widened and her hands moved across her belly. She looked as though she were holding her child in her arms and praying for its well-being. As I started the same song that I had sung the evening before, the doorway became full of strangers, peering inside like a gathering of lost souls. This time there was no whispering. I could only hear the sound of my voice echoing off the bleak walls. When I was done, there was no crying, laughing or cheering. There was silence. And after I looked up at the young girl's bruised body, I showed myself out the door. No one stopped me or even questioned it. They knew I was the 'American' – the girl who had it all.

We left shortly after that. I wanted to. I don't know why I wanted to go. Maybe it was because I still didn't understand. The *gitanos* are rare and beautiful. I never spoke to them but I felt them. I didn't feel what they were going through – I never could have. But I felt something. And that was that it takes much more than words to communicate.

18

The Speaking Barrier

Amelia Villagómez

As I open the refrigerator door I see my grandfather standing behind me. I look down at him as he looks up at me. He doesn't even have to speak. I see the disappointment in his eyes. In silence I am chastised. He does not even utter those all-too familiar words: 'You should make time for a Persian lesson; you are behind.' I can't look at him any longer. With my eyes gazing down at the carpet I recently vacuumed, I go to my room to analyze my misery.

I take out my Persian book, hidden behind my geometry book and a migraine-producing science book. Next I find that spiral notebook containing my years of Persian lessons. In a sense, that notebook has been my confidant – always ready for me to begin, patient during my absence and always providing me with a fresh start. That spiral has endured fits and tantrums, long periods of emptiness when I gave up and success when I finally tried.

Eventually I get out a pencil. Dull point. I gotta sharpen it. My grandfather is very meticulous and won't let me write with something that his aged eyes can't read. Ready? No, my mind wanders. It's a beautiful day outside. The house awaits my sturdy sweeper and rag. Oh, and I still have to write that essay on the French and Indian War that was due last Friday. So much to do. Yet I'm stuck in my room, staring at the ceiling fan circulating the guilt I feel throughout my aching and tired body. I begin to write the title of my assignment and my mind travels to the life of my grandfather.

My grandfather was raised in Bombay, India, and learned to speak Hindi. When he was three, his family moved to Iran, where he remained most of his life. There he became well-acquainted with the Persian language. He was a wonderful speaker and poet. He could recite poems and even complete those impossible crossword puzzles printed in the Persian newspapers. He raised five children and sent them to America to further their studies. The point is that he was an accomplished poet, father and teacher of the Faith of Bahá'u'lláh.

At the age of 58 my grandfather left his friends in Iran, everything he knew and everything he spent his life building, to see his children and grandchildren in America. By leaving Iran he left his life of true communication. When he came to America, he couldn't understand English. When he watched television he only understood facial expressions – the words uttered were foreign to him. He entered a world where most of his communication had to be non-verbal. His only links to his native language were his family and his specially made radio which could get two Persian-speaking stations. His Persian radio, as we called it, was on continually during the day and into the late hours of the night; sometimes he even slept with it turned on.

America is a wonderful place. There are computers, telephones, cars, ovens and fans. It's affordable, comfortable and great. We have rights that give us freedom according to the constitution. Yet, are you 'free' if you walk downtown and can't understand a word that anyone says? Are you 'free' if you can't understand what someone says on the telephone? Are you 'free' when you turn on the television and can't understand what the reporters are saying? Sure you have freedom of speech but if no one can understand you, what is the purpose? How can you be 'free'? You are imprisoned in a society that doesn't understand you.

My grandfather is a unique jewel yet if he can't be understood, how can he express his uniqueness?

Now me. There are so many things I could be doing other than educating myself in language. Yes, it is important to be multilingual but I wish language didn't matter.

One of the teachings of the Bahá'í religion is that in the future there should be a one universal language in addition to one's own mother tongue. If a universal language were a reality now, my grandfather could still express himself in Persian when he was around those who understand Persian and he could speak in the universal language when he was around those who don't. The whole world would be more unified if we all could share ideas directly without the errors of translation and miscommunication.

My grandfather is truly beautiful. In a way he has created a unique language. Although I can understand his words, his unique non-verbal language is more communicative. It is a language of actions and expressions. I am more fluent in this language of his. I can tell the mood he is in just by the way his eyebrows are positioned, the way he flips a card at his game of solitaire or simply by how he walks or chants. Sometimes I can sit with him in complete silence and we can understand each other.

Sometimes I think words are a barrier to communication. Not all feelings can be expressed in words and sometimes when we do put them into words, they are misunderstood or underestimated. True language is a language of actions, when few words are spoken and many actions are carried out. A world of words is simply a mundane world of monotony. Yet if we develop these two languages within ourselves, the verbal and nonverbal, we can change the way the world works. I think we need to talk less and have more positive actions. Words are great, yet they cannot stand alone. Words linked with actions form a bridge of love and communication.

19

Brazilerican

An Interview with Sara Isabel Vargas Lawrence by Sandy Nosseir

S ara Isabel Vargas Lawrence, 20 when this was written, is half
Costa Rican and half American. Both of her parents are of
Portuguese descent. She is a dancer and was born in Costa Rica.
Having lived in both Arizona and New York, at the time of this inter-
view she lived in Brazil as an exchange student from Sarah Lawrence
College. She was interviewed in New York when she was on a break
from her year of study in Brazil. I sat down with her to explore her
thoughts on culture and her exposure to Brazilian ways of life.

Sandy: Tell me a little about your ethnic background. How long did
you live in Costa Rica?

Sara: I lived in Costa Rica until I was five and I have visited since
then. The majority of the population is *mestizo* or ethnically
mixed. There's also a small population descended from Africans
who came to the Caribbean concentrated along the Atlantic coast.
Many retired Europeans and Americans live there also. I found
the same diversity within families there. I remember having a
neighbor who had two daughters, the eldest had darker skin and
tight curly hair while the younger one had long hair and blue
eyes. Basically, throughout Latin America you have the same
three elements that contribute to the mix: the descendants of the
African slaves, the native Indians and finally the Europeans. It's
basically the same mix in varying degrees.

Sandy: How does being of mixed ethnic backgrounds affect you and
how do you identify yourself?

Sara: Coming from two different cultures is a big issue here in the
States. Here, I feel everyone wants to know what you are. You're
either this or you're that and you can't really be both. If you do

choose to claim both, some people will look down on you because
there are certain connotations that go with every culture. But
when I stop to think about the way my parents raised me, it was
with Bahá'í culture. For instance, I really can't say I am Hispanic
because a lot of that culture is tied to the Church. So there are
aspects of that which are lacking in my upbringing. Perhaps when
we lived in Costa Rica my ethnic identity was stronger but once
we came to the States that disappeared and the only thing I held
onto was the language, which I had to struggle to keep. When
I go back to Costa Rica I feel different from my cousins. Yet I
always feel different back here too. My culture has been in limbo,
so it has been hard to distinguish what I am. My parents have
done an incredible job in fusing their cultures together to the
point that they are almost indistinguishable. So maybe that's why
people sometimes can't tell what I am. When I was growing up I
went to powwows on the Indian reservations in Arizona and to
Persian dinners. It was very varied. So that's my culture, that's
my upbringing, that's what I know. It's all based around being a
world citizen, which is what it means to be a Bahá'í. That's how I
identify myself.

Sandy: Having grown up in Costa Rica, were there aspects of the
culture that you feel affected your value system?

Sara: Definitely. It's Latin in many ways but I learned something
new in Sáo Paulo. When I went to Brazil I wanted to believe I
was more Latin than American. But being there made me realize
how American I am. I was in this strange country without any
reference points, knowledge of the language, etc. While I was
there, I found that I bonded more with the other Americans.
Everyone in the group I was there with was very different from
each other and I know that in the States none of us would have
been friends. Even though there are racial and cultural barriers
between people here in the States, I realized how much of a bond
I have with other Americans, even if I can only talk about the
hamburgers at McDonald's or the movies that came out last week.
In a way that's our culture – things that we can all refer to. These
things all contribute to something deeper, a mentality, a way of

thinking. Here everything is very convenient and that creates a certain culture. When you go somewhere else and the rhythm is completely different, you realize how many things contribute to American culture. For example, there are traditions in the US that you won't find in other countries. When I lived in Costa Rica we didn't celebrate Thanksgiving, of course. But when we moved here, we began celebrating it. It seems that people adapt to the traditions and culture of the place where they live.

Sandy: Does this mean part of your Latin culture was compromised or that it took a back seat to American culture?

Sara: Well, even though everyone celebrates Thanksgiving in the States, it is very different in each household. The turkey may be the only common element left on everyone's dinner table because of the influence of Latino heritage, for instance. As a side note, in the 1920s a Brazilian artist who felt that the Brazilians had copied European culture for too long developed a theory. He proposed that the Brazilians take the good of all other cultures and Brazilianize it. I think this happens anyway when someone moves from one country to another. They may accept certain aspects of the second culture but their own culture can influence it, creating something new. People of South American descent celebrating Thanksgiving in the US may have a Thanksgiving with *arroz con pollo* – chicken with rice. It may not be mashed potatoes and cranberry sauce but it is their Thanksgiving.

Sandy: What was your experience bringing your American culture to Brazil?

Sara: In Brazil there's a sort of love-hate feeling towards America. If you're not American you are on their side, which is good in a way. But still, to be American is this all-glorious thing. I mean, I had never seen so many McDonald's in my life before I went to Brazil. And they are always crowded. The radio stations there also play a lot of American music. In many ways they look up to Americans for all the things they have but at the same time there is still a feeling of 'us' versus 'them'. That's why they use the term *gringos*. Americans come off very cocky, very arrogant, 'We are the best.'

Well, okay but when you stop and think, when you go to Brazil, Brazilians know more about your culture than you do. How much do Americans know about theirs? Brazilians have seen all of our movies and they can speak our language. So I feel that the world knows everything about America but America knows nothing about the world around it. It was quite humbling to be there, to say the least.

Sandy: How much of a role do you think race plays in Brazilian culture?

Sara: One thing I heard a lot in Brazil is that racism doesn't exist there because of a tradition of intermixing since the colonists arrived. They were all too happy to mix with the locals. So there's been about 400 years of this mixing of the races and in Brazil you see such a diversity among the people, within a family and in the country at large.

Sandy: Did you find it true that racism doesn't exist there?

Sara: To some extent it's true. Superficially, people do get along more and there's more friendliness between the races than, let's say, here in America. But in some ways it's bad because everyone is sort of in denial about it. Racism very much exists there but people seem to just accept it as being part of life. It's more subtle and it's based more on class.

Sandy: How so?

Sara: When you look at who has what job and who has the money, it's the people who are lighter. I noticed on my plane ride here that all the Brazilians who were flying looked like Europeans. When you walk into an office building, the people who work as janitors and maids are people of color. What's also interesting to consider is the fact that Brazil has a large population of people who are out of work. In their desperation to provide for their families they are willing to work for almost nothing. Many of the women migrate to São Paulo and are hired as maids. Everybody there has a maid. It's almost like the maids have maids. It's this continuous system of someone serving someone else. The maids (or *fashineras,* as they call them) are all darker than the people they work for. So inter-racial marriages alone don't put an end to prejudice. Prejudice can exist on many different levels.

Sandy: Considering your multi-ethnic background and your experiences in other countries, how important do you consider race to be?

Sara: What's nice is that my ethnic background and upbringing have given me exposure to so many different and wonderful cultures. This has enabled me to relate to many different people. Many of the things my parents integrated into my childhood weren't even from their cultures. It was just because they were Bahá'ís and that was part of the experience they wanted me to have.

What am I? This is something I have asked myself often. When I stop to think about it I realize I have been raised in a Bahá'í culture. When I look back at all the influences, I realize that there has been nothing completely Costa Rican, nothing completely American and nothing completely Portuguese. So you see, you can become psychotic trying to figure out what you are. I think that in the grand scheme of things, it's not really that important. You can't define race and culture in black and white terms. I can't put my experience in one definitive box. In some way I'd have to be untruthful if I was forced to categorize myself. I am glad I have been raised this way because I can now befriend a wide variety of people. Others can't do this because they confine themselves to these little spaces.

Sandy: Considering the cultural and racial conflicts which exist throughout the world, what are your thoughts on world peace?

Sara: First of all, having traveled out of the country, I have learned that the human spirit is the same everywhere. The only thing that's different is people's experiences. I can see why some people doubt that the unity of humanity is possible. But I think that we need to humble ourselves more in order to enter the lands of other people and truly understand them. It is when we can understand where everybody is coming from that we can truly celebrate the oneness of mankind!

20

Culture Crash

An Interview with Soo-Jin Yoon by Aaron Emmel

Soo-Jin Yoon, 27 at the time of this interview, has traveled all over the world and it seems that wherever she goes she immediately impresses and befriends everyone she meets. What is her secret? How is she able to manage so well in such a variety of cultures? These are some of the questions I asked Soo-Jin at her apartment in Albuquerque, New Mexico.

Aaron: How long have you been a Bahá'í?

Soo-Jin: I've been a Bahá'í for over eight years. I was studying at the University of Illinois in my sophomore year. I had a lot of questions about religion: 'How could a just God let a world run like this?' and things like that. The person who taught me – and the way she taught – was perfect for me. Basically, she just slowly introduced me to the Faith without teaching me outright.

Aaron: Was this Layla?

Soo-Jin: Layla, yes. I had been given the *Hidden Words* at a fireside she took me to and in the back was a quotation of 'Abdu'l-Bahá, 'Be a lamp, be as a Bahá'í'. I started memorizing it, just to keep my mind off my problems. Soon after that I talked with Layla until five in the morning. I asked her all the questions I had left, like, 'What about people who drink because it's part of their culture?' In the end, what Layla said was that the most important thing was that you believe in Bahá'u'lláh and the teachings and everything else is secondary. I was like, okay, I guess I don't really have any reason that I shouldn't be a Bahá'í!

Aaron: What made you take that step?

Soo-Jin: I think the thing that touched me the most was realizing how sacred, how important and how special the Bahá'í Faith was to the Bahá'ís I had met.

Aaron: What did the Bahá'í Faith mean to you then?

Soo-Jin: It wasn't that special to me at that point because I had just learned about it and so I felt weird about saying I was a Bahá'í. I was sort of worried about it. It was a matter-of-fact kind of declaration. And then a couple days later, Layla cried and I didn't understand why. A few days after that she gave me a declaration card and I signed it. I was reading about things and I knew a lot of facts. I knew that what I loved about the Bahá'í Faith were the principles. I watched the Bahá'ís striving to meet those standards and their everyday struggles and I really admired them for that. That's what I liked but I don't think I ever truly understood the magnitude of Bahá'u'lláh's Revelation or what the Revelation was until I went teaching, which was about four months after I became a Bahá'í. I went down to Belize.

Aaron: Why did you decide to go travel teaching to another country so soon?

Soo-Jin: I don't really know. When you take that step and sign the declaration card, things start happening. Half the time I didn't know what was going to happen. I couldn't have imagined how I was going to change or what it meant to go travel teaching. I think I was guided, like being enrolled in the Bahá'í school, I guess. I was given crash courses and was pushed along.

At first I wanted to travel and experience something outside of the US, so I started looking at employment because I didn't have money. I paid 30 dollars for a list of places to work and I wrote to them but no one wrote back. Then Layla said, 'Why don't you try travel teaching?' And I was like, Oh, okay, all right! I wrote to the National Center and they gave me some information. I picked three or four countries where they spoke English – Botswana, Belize and a couple other countries – and I decided on Belize because it was the closest and the least expensive.

Aaron: Very important considerations.

Soo-Jin: And I had NO idea what the heck I was doing. But I never really worried.

I remember at one point when I was about to leave, my mom asked me, 'Well, what are you going to do if no one comes to get you, if no one's there to meet you at the airport?' It never dawned on me to think like that. I didn't even have addresses or phone numbers. I just knew that someone was going to meet me at the airport. I think part of it was me. I wanted to improve myself as far as being a Bahá'í was concerned. But I think there are two ways you can be deepened in knowledge of the Bahá'í Faith – you can have the intellectual deepening and then you have a totally different, almost mysterious, mystical sense of spiritual deepening, where you're guided to the things you need to learn and the stuff you need to have. I think I was definitely pushed in that direction. When I got to Belize, I couldn't have asked for anything better. Now that I've been a Bahá'í for a number of years, I've heard stories of how people go to countries and they're not prepared or there are a lot of difficulties. Obviously I was protected. Belize is one of the most nurturing countries, now that I look at it. The people there just took me in. I call Belize my spiritual mother country because that was where I *really* learned about the Bahá'í Faith.

Aaron: How old were you when you went to Belize?

Soo-Jin: I was 19.

Aaron: So what actually happened when you were there?

Soo-Jin: Well, someone met me at the airport! Bob Hutchcraft. Bob was this jolly, big man who came up to me and just hugged me. It took me by surprise. He's as white as you can get. Then there was a really black lady, Beverly. She was from Jamaica and was travel teaching. They drove me over to Counsellor Ahmadiyeh's house – he and his family lived in Belize City. I had no idea that I was in the presence of a very important person. He passed away a couple years after that. Then we drove to the capital, Belmopan, and went through two or three days of orientation. They taught me how to teach, went through the teaching goals and deepened me. And it was all new to me, I mean, everything was new to me and I was so nervous.

Aaron: How did they 'teach you how to teach'?

Soo-Jin: We did role playing with Beverly, pretending that she was teaching me, and I had to try to turn around and do it. I swear, I must have repeated exactly how she taught, every word, every example, every analogy, because I had never heard any of that before. I remember at one point that it came up that Bahá'u'lláh was the return of Christ. See, before that, I had understood the unity of the Manifestations. I had understood that all the Prophets talked about the Prophets of the future but I had never really thought about it – and no one had ever said it to me in those words – that Bahá'u'lláh was the return of Christ. When that came up, since I had been a Christian before, it was a big shocker. I didn't say anything to anybody but I was thinking, 'My God, what are these people saying? They're saying that He's the return of Christ! Isn't that, like, huge news?'

Aaron: Were you comfortable being so suddenly immersed in such a new environment and new world view?

Soo-Jin: I was going through a lot internally. Especially there. The whole time I didn't say anything but I was very nervous. I thought, these people are so dedicated and they're sacrificing everything. They're out here doing all this stuff and here I am, I'm supposed to be an assistant or a help to them. But I am so afraid that I am a burden, that they have to take care of me and that I am imposing and being more of a burden than a help. I really struggled with that – that was the big test for the summer: realizing that whatever effort you put in, no matter how little you know, no matter how inadequate you feel, it's still up to Bahá'u'lláh.

Aaron: So what was it like going out to the villages and teaching?

Soo-Jin: Well, when I was 19 I didn't want to be surprised by anything. You think you know everything and you can handle everything, especially around college time, and you want to be adventurous. I just took in everything and thought, 'Oh, yeah, that's the way it's supposed to be.' I think for some people it might have been a big shock because of the conditions and the physical hardships but at that point nothing fazed me. I think being the age that I was, with everything being so new and me having just become a Bahá'í, I was there to soak everything up. I look back now and think, 'Oh my God, how did I do it?'

Aaron: Describe some of those conditions.

Soo-Jin: I remember traveling from town to town. I'd get on these buses – half the time you don't have a seat and the roads are so bumpy. You're standing there and you have nothing to grab onto and you're between all these sweaty people and it's so hot and it's so dusty. When I got off the bus I'd scratch my nails across my skin, my face, and I would have caked-on mud under my nails. It's so humid, you're sweating and everything just sticks to you. It was very dirty. Actually, I struggled with this.

Before we went out to the villages I did a little travel teaching with Beverly. We were partners. We traveled down south and met up with a lot of other people. It was the beginning of the summer and there was a summer institute being held, followed by a teaching project. So we all met up and we had this institute – there were probably 40 or 50 of us. From there, we were all assigned a teacher and a group – teams of teachers went to different towns. A drama and dance group went from town to town. Part of our role as teachers was to prepare for the performances and the teaching, that kind of thing.

There were the other goals, like setting up children's classes, training teachers and holding Feasts. I got assigned to this little tiny town, and when I realized where I was assigned, I sort of freaked out because I knew it was going to be hard. I wanted to be with the youth because I was young. I didn't say anything but at one point I was almost teary-eyed and I told myself, 'Soo-Jin, calm down. There's a reason why you're going there and you'll just accept it.' It just took me five minutes and I totally accepted it. Then we got there and after the bus ride the first thing I wanted to do was take a shower. Of course there was no running water, no electricity, nothing. Just mosquitoes and sand flies.

Aaron: Mosquitoes seem to be everywhere in Central America.

Soo-Jin: And sand flies like crazy. The first week I was there I had so many sand fly and mosquito bites. Just on one leg, from my knee down to my ankle, I counted over 110 bites. It was horrible. I get very allergic reactions. I was walking around and trying to wear loose clothing. When it gets hot the bites get very irritating, so I was walking around like this the whole time. I still have scars from them. Other people didn't get bitten as badly – for some reason I was being initiated or something.

  Anyway, we got there and secured a place to stay but then the guys on the team had to find another place and it was getting late and dark. There was no electricity. Now that I think about it, these are really sweet memories but at the time, you're just like, whoa!

Aaron: 'How did I get into this?'

Soo-Jin: Yeah! I remember I had made sure to bring a little cushion to sleep on and one of the guys didn't have one, so I gave mine to him. I said I could sleep on the hammock, which was hanging in the house. All these houses are built on sticks because they are on sand. I tried to sleep in the hammock but couldn't do it, so I ended up on the floor and there were ants crawling all over me, cockroaches crawling all over me. But I was so tired that I just thought, 'Okay.'

  And then they brought us two buckets, one to go to the bathroom in and the other bucket to wash up in; it had water in it. They put it in the kitchen area but by mistake the guys locked the kitchen before they went, so we couldn't even go to the bathroom or wash up. We had to go outside. You couldn't see anything, it was so dark. We just went out and squatted. And then I realized, later, after I'd stayed there for a while, that the local people are so used to having no electricity that they walk around all the time in the dark. So anybody could have been walking around at that time. The next morning, I looked at the water and I was so glad I hadn't bathed in it because it was brown. They said it was only minerals but I thought it was really disgusting.

The people in the village were so different from the people in the bigger towns of Belize. With all these personal struggles, it took me a while to figure out how I was going to relate to them. I had a difficult time until I realized we're all one people, just of different kinds with different cultures. I had to try to change little things, like the way I approached people. It was an experience. I ran into everything from scorpions to chopped-up cat claws.

Aaron: How were you able to relate to the people around you?

Soo-Jin: You just try to find ways. I've seen the materials from the National Spiritual Assembly and National Teaching Committee about how you have to be aware of your own culture and ethnocentrism and how you should try to imagine things from other people's culture, see it from their perspective and not judge. I think those skills are good on one level but the most important thing is love. As long as you feel you love the people you're in contact with, no matter what cultural differences or difficulties you have, people can see it. Especially pure-hearted people from the villages – they can detect sincerity, they can detect condescension, they can sense it much more than we can. But I remember really struggling with it.

I once watched a group of Mayan women, up the river, washing clothes. We had to do all our bathing and washing in the river. I sat there, thinking, 'Oh my God, how do I start, what do I say to them, how do I talk to them?' You know? But it's just a matter of getting used to it and being comfortable with yourself. And finding things out about other people which are interesting to you. There's always the commonality of children. You can ask about their children, about their health or what's happening in the community, things like that. But like I said, most important is love. No matter what, you need to sincerely love the person and love the people that you're teaching. You need to have the attitude of service rather than 'I'm here to teach you something' because obviously that doesn't work. And I think you need to pray, pray for the station of servitude and pray for love.

21

Thai Tea Thief

Aixa Maria Sobin

The tall glass of tea was cold, making my Boston-winter hands even colder. The huge chunks of ice banged against my lips as I sipped the orangey concoction, making it difficult for me to take big gulps. Scooping out the ice and relishing the last few sips, I ordered another one, this time with no ice. The more Thai tea I drank, the more I was satisfied. I was not satisfying thirst but the craving to be there again, to have, to take, to steal the moments back.

I wanted to squish red Om Goi village mud between my toes. To play volleyball with the small village children while we took a class break next to their one-room straw-built schoolhouse. To dance on the slippery concrete floors of the performance hall in Nongkai – where I gave one of the best dance performances of my life to youth from all over Southeast Asia. To curtsey to the smiles of the teachers I visited and trained in Yasothon. To see youth in Chiangmai become transformed as I shared the 15-Method Theater project. But in the last gulp I was thinking of Tawa. There is nowhere else like Tawa. Somehow I had to find a way to return to the village of Tawa; that place, that shack, that fishing village and that tea. That summer-hot tea that introduced me to my new Thai family. This tea, this Boston Back Bay Thai restaurant tea, which smelled and tasted very little like the land of Thailand, was the closest I was going to get for now.

I was no longer teaching just inside the borders of Macau. I was no longer traveling, training teachers and giving youth workshops all over Southeast Asia. I was back in Boston, back where I thought I belonged, and a round trip ticket to return to Thailand would certainly be more than the $150 I had. I was too far away . . . three months away from those moments. Three months later and my reason for coming back home was still not clear. Three months later and I still did not have a job. Three months later and I had failed to show to all my old friends the new person Thailand had helped me to become. Three months . . . without washing Khun's glasses. I wondered what Khun thought of me.

My voice raised high, I said, 'Kapkunkaa', stretching the last vowel for five seconds (making my accent sound authentic), as I received the tea from my waitress, who smiled and giggled in approval. The spiced tea and cream flavors were a gift to my mouth; I didn't want to swallow. I would hold each gulp for a moment, not wanting to let it go . . . thinking of her face. Dreaming of receiving another one of the full-bodied, life-giving, Thai-mother embraces Khun had rendered me before I left her tea shop in Tawa to go back to Songcla on my way to Hong Kong to catch my plane to America. I love Tawa and tea only because of Khun.

My old friend had not stopped talking since we had walked into the restaurant. He was excited to see me again after so many years but this evening I was in a world of tea. I marveled at the colors . . . as the white, the cream, the orange, the tea blended together. Without stirring, the white slowly ran down into the bottom, without a fight. The white, as it infiltrates the tea, stretches itself, forming zig-zags and squiggles of color in my glass. Although separate entities in the beginning, they end up one: one color, one taste, one sweet and delicious tea. This statement of color, of taste, of unity, not only made me think of Khun but somehow made me question who I was. Who am I? I am always asked.

As I stole the last orange drops from my tall glass, I ordered another. My hands, which were also reminiscing, lost their sense of time and place, left me in the Boston restaurant and dunked themselves in her sink. They were in Tawa, in the sun-heated, detergentless water of the sink in Khun's stall. The water where I had rinsed and washed all her miniature Thai glasses covered with remnants of her sweet tea recipe. I rinsed and washed them with plain water; there was no soap, so I scrubbed them hard. I set them upside down on the dark wooden handmade counter top, which was water-stained from years of cleaning the cups of satisfied customers.

The race began. The more cups I dunked and bathed, the more people ordered tea. I could never accumulate enough cups to feel like I was really getting anywhere. Khun would gather cups in one big swoop and pour the orange stuff with such grace that her hands seemed to be conducting a choir instead of pouring tea. Khun was getting to the end of the clean glasses when she smiled at me, grabbed the small, black, square tub, threw the water into a crevice on the street and filled the tub again with water from a wooden cylindrical vat.

Shoppers kept walking in, their hands full with their morning market goods, and occupied every stool. I enjoyed looking back and catching a glimpse every once in a while, since my back was to the sitting customers. Khun needed more glasses and I, as her new family member, her new daughter, was not going to let her down. I stayed focused, and tried to ignore the people who were watching me clean the glasses, wondering if Westerners used different methods. I tried not to correct all the English words people were practicing with me as they passed by. I stayed calm in front of those faces that got intimately close to me, wondering where I was from (as people from around the world often wonder).

The race continued. I changed the water every 30 glasses. I washed and rinsed each one for five Mississippis . . . and at this pace I began to catch up. As Khun checked on me, she motheringly slapped my back with her fluffy, soft, cool, damp hands, a blessing under the hot sun.

The chitter-chatter of the shoppers got louder and there were almost two dozen motor-propelled canoes docked by the land's edge. Someone's watch beeped 8:00 a.m. and I dumped another batch of dirty water. As I looked up I saw equal amounts of clean and orange-spotted glasses. I was happy. My hands looked decades older than my face, my Bangkok silk blue blouse was covered with splatters and my feet were throbbing (they never like standing in one place for too long) – but I was serving my new mom. Khun had adopted me on my first trip to Tawa, the night after the hurricane.

I had come to Khun's stall to have some tea and to eat sticky rice and deep fried chicken and onions. I had approached that particular stall because it seemed like a nice, quiet place to relax from the early morning marketing. I had a mouth full of tea and a big chicken wing when the owner of the shop came to talk to me in his broken English.

He introduced himself as the English teacher in the local elementary school and his wife, Khun, as the brilliant tea-maker. Somehow during our conversation over a couple of glasses of complimentary tea, Khun decided to adopt me. Khun's husband translated his wife's wishes and I agreed. There was no ceremony, no party, only a light slap on my back from my new mom as she smiled deeply from my resounding 'yes'. For some reason they had never been able to have children, so I had to make sure to be a good daughter and help them any way I could. I did not want to give them a bad impression of daughters. And this – this was the reason for washing Khun's glasses and doing the best job possible.

I finished all the glasses as the stream of customers began to slow down. I sat down on the weather-beaten wooden stool and was brought a complimentary glass of tea, hot straight up. This was my tea . . . this was my family. My adopted parents smiled at me, so proud of my speedy hands. They looked so beautiful holding each other amidst the vapors of the tea and coffee and the crowds of shoppers swarming in and around their restaurant to the music of hooting cars and motorcycles and the occasional singing roosters and chickens.

But being part of their family did not mean that I had relinquished mine. This act did not mean that I had abandoned my Russian English Jewish Spanish Black Puerto Rican family ancestry but had somehow added to it. This supplemented my culture, my sense of being, my sense of self – contributing flavor and color to my cultural tea, creating a unique and spicy blend. No one could separate it into all its varied components. Just like no one can separate Thai tea.

While I drank my fourth cup of tea, the waitress came to me, nervous and obviously embarrassed, and said that they did not have any 'Som Tam Thai'. But before she walked away from me, we whispered to each other the names of all our favorite Thai dishes this American Thai restaurant did not serve. So I resigned myself to Pad Thai. Although warm, sweet and delicious, especially on a Boston-cold winter stomach, it is not one of the most popular dishes among the villagers of Thailand with whom I spent time.

After I curtsied to the wait-staff, with my legs and palms together and knees bent, in the respectable, old-fashioned Thai style, I left the restaurant and waved goodbye to my friend as he turned around the corner. My hands were damp and cold and my feet were throbbing.

I sat down on the C line train and closed my eyes in exhaustion from the trip I had just taken. But I opened them up to joy. I could hear conversations being carried on in Mandarin, Cantonese, Spanish, English . . . and melodic Thai. Although simultaneous, and in different tones, pitches and voice levels, I could hear them all. Too tired to respond or reveal my language-knowledge, I sat like a spy, a thief, stealing their words, their laughter, their conversations. All of them being robbed without knowledge simply because my face, my skin, my eyes could not give me away.

So who am I? Am I really a thief, as some have implied? Am I a thief because I adopt cultural rituals, codes of behavior, norms, manners, dress, eating patterns, languages and systems of beliefs from each and every country I have lived, worked and traveled in? Or are these part of my heritage?

Is this where society is heading? Will society become a fusion of cultures, so blended, so infused, that we can no longer recall where any behavior, manner, food, word came from?

Aren't we like that already?

22

Mango

Karim Beers

The fruit of the mango tree is usually about the size of an apple but it may weigh as much as three pounds. It consists of a soft, juicy, lush yellow or orange pulp and has a delicious, sweet and spicy flavor.

The mere recollection of its delectable pulp makes me salivate profusely. The mango has a single large pit with fleshy strands growing out of it into the pulp. Nature has made the pit such that it works excellently as an adult's pacifier: it fits perfectly into the mouth, tastes great and you can chew on it and pull on the long strands forever – at least until enough fibers get caught in between your teeth that it becomes unbearable and you are forced to floss.

Imagine: a fleshy fruit in which sweetness, spice and texture are perfectly harmonized – in essence, 100 per cent oral satisfaction. The mango is my favorite fruit.

There are about 500 mango varieties. Perhaps this explains the vast fluctuations in the taste of mangos. One mango can send my oral senses flying into seventh heaven, while another may merely earn a free ticket to the compost. However, the taste of the former is enough to keep me gambling and I freely give my passionate devotion to this fruit of fruits.

How strange! Though I'm more than willing to shower compliments on a fruit, I don't even stop to mention the virtues of its rightful owner and maker – the mango tree. It seems rather unfair to dedicate all my attention to the edible product of a tree and yet not give due credit to the 'brain' behind the scenes. It is as if I were paying compliments to a house for its beauty yet completely neglecting to praise the architect or carpenter! Or congratulating the president for giving a wonderful inauguration speech, when in fact he didn't write a word of it!

The mango tree *is* very attractive. It is thick and dark green, an evergreen at that. The tree has slender, pointed leaves about one foot long. Tiny pink flowers grow in clusters, adorning the ends of small branches. The tree can grow to the amazing height of 50 feet but unfortunately mango trees grow only in the tropics, thus we Ithacans remain deprived of the beauty of the tree. We can, however, eat mangoes – thanks to the trade relations among nations – if we are willing to pay the exorbitant price of a dollar plus per fruit.

Last year I lived in Israel. I dwelled north of the two big cities, Tel Aviv and Jerusalem, in the third largest Israeli city, Haifa, and I breathed the salty Mediterranean air. I worked as a gardener, caring for the thousands of trees in the ornamental gardens of the Bahá'í World Centre. About 700 other Bahá'í volunteers serve there in different capacities: either maintaining the buildings and grounds or carrying on the office duties at the spiritual and administrative center of the Bahá'í Faith. The volunteers come from many different cultures and countries: St Helena, the Philippines, Portugal, New Zealand, Costa Rica, Uganda, India, Nepal and Canada, to name but a few. I personally was blessed with Akwetey, my roommate from Ghana.

I don't think a better companion could have been found, for we were complete opposites! He slept on the floor in the living room – or on any other open surface – and I chose my bed. He liked to sleep with a light on and I had no chance of sleeping if there was any light in my vicinity. I loved to have the windows open; he liked them closed, due in part to the occasional stone tossed by the children who were our neighbors. I liked classical music; he liked '70s pop (though we both loved Tracy Chapman). And the list goes on: he loved meat dishes and I preferred vegetarian . . .

Akwetey is the most pure-hearted person I have ever known. He was also a complete enigma to me. While I could understand his British/African accent – 'milk' was 'muk' and 'bird' was 'bed' – some things about him I could not understand.

Akwetey always liked doing things with others: cooking, eating, walking to the garden to work, going to talks, visiting the holy places, shopping, playing soccer – you name it, he liked company. Naturally, to an independence-loving, solitary young American male, this seemed very strange. It was completely the opposite of what I thought to be appropriate behavior. However, my affection surpassed my discomfort, so I'd usually end up alongside Akwetey, arm in arm, walking down the narrow stairs of Haifa. On occasion, after a long day of work pruning citrus trees or planting cypress, we'd walk home together, deviating from our usual path in order to pass by a small kiosk at the end of our street.

The shopkeeper, a Christian Arab, was a very warm and friendly person; he would always give us a good deal on fruit and pitta bread (or so we chose to think). During the summer we often bought watermelon from his shop for about 1.5 shekels a kilo and we served the watermelon at parties we threw for the other Bahá'í youth in the area. We actually became well-known among these youth for the delectable and sticky feasts we held in our humble home! This fame, however, was short-lived. As watermelon season came to a close, prices of this commodity rose, the quality of the fruit declined and we stopped buying the melon. We started looking around for a new fruit to fill the space on our table and in our stomachs.

Fortunately, mango season began and our search for fruit was ended. In a short time we developed such a liking for this fruit that we even structured rituals around it. Akwetey would frequently buy mangoes in secret and hide them in the fridge. He would then wait until we were home together, look at me – making sure he made eye contact – and raise his eyebrows a few times. As I nodded in a sign of recognition, he'd smile. We'd walk together to the fridge, look each other in the eye and smile a very sly and conniving smile: it was time to feast.

Akwetey frequently worked long hours in the section of gardens he was in charge of, sometimes laboring from dawn to dusk in order to finish a job he had started. On those days I would arrive home to an empty apartment and would take my time showering, dressing, cleaning up and awaiting Akwetey's return. On occasion I would open the fridge, look around, take out a mango, peel it, slice it and eat it (saving the pit for last, of course). However, I would do this infrequently, for I always found the mango to be a little too sweet, a bit too hard or too bitter.

Whatever made those mangoes sweet, Akwetey had something to do with it. I noticed something similar when I rented the video of *Sense and Sensibility* some weeks ago. I had high expectations, for I had watched *Pride and Prejudice* in Israel and loved it with a passion. However, when I began to watch *Sense and Sensibility* by myself, I found little enjoyment and turned the TV off. I waited until my family came home from school and work and I watched it together with them. I was quite diverted this time around, though I did not derive as much enjoyment as I had in Israel when ten of us were packed into a small room: Indian, Persian, Costa Rican and Filipino Bahá'ís actively trying to understand what the characters were saying and commenting freely when the characters needed some advice. The diversity of the people, coupled with the unity of purpose watching the movie, made an effective and unique whole. The potential for joy was increased exponentially by the diversity of cultures, releasing much more zest than the sum of the individual parts might do. Like the roots, leaves and branches of a tree, our union contributed to the making of a fruit. A sweet fruit, a fruit of enjoyment and conviviality.

I crossed the Atlantic Ocean and returned home some months ago. I haven't eaten a mango since. Perhaps I will wait for Akwetey; he hopes to visit soon. I can picture us now: an African and an American getting together to partake of the sweetest Southeast Asian fruit.

23

Transformation

An Interview with Houman Vafai by Roddy Khadem

Roddy: How long have you been a Bahá'í?

Houman: I was born into a Bahá'í family. I grew up in Iran until I was about seven. At that time both my parents were fired from their jobs because we were Bahá'ís. My mom was a doctor, my dad an engineer. We were living a comfortable life. My parents were given the option to recant their faith or leave the country. One of the fundamentals of belief, in my opinion, is that you stick with it, no matter what forces are in opposition.

Roddy: How old are you now?

Houman: I'm 20 years old. It's been about 13 years that I've been in America. I was born in Isfahan. When we were leaving the country because of religious persecution, I actually didn't know because I was a child. My parents didn't tell me we were leaving. I guess I was too young to understand that I was leaving my friends and going to another country. My parents just said, 'We're going on a trip.' They were crying but my sister and brother and I didn't know. My brother was only one year old. After a little while, I found out that we were not coming back. Our first stop was Pakistan.

Roddy: Your brother was one, you were seven and how old was your sister?

Houman: My sister was nine. We went to Pakistan and there we were escorted by a Pakistani tribe. We paid them to take us across the border.

Roddy: What was the trip like, going from Isfahan to Pakistan? Was there emotional turmoil?

Houman: The whole trip was nothing like a normal trip, where you take a bus and then you take a plane somewhere else. This was an escape, not the normal route people take to get out of Iran. We had to get a truck and that was our main source of transportation. We had to go through back valleys and deserts. I remember that my mom, brother and sister were in the front seat of the truck and my dad and I were in the bed of the pick-up. We had to lie down so the officers who were stationed in the mountains and the deserts wouldn't see us. We also had to dress up as members of the tribe. It wasn't pants and shirts; it was a distinct outfit that showed that we were associated with the tribe.

Roddy: Tell me about the trip from Pakistan. Where did you go from there?

Houman: We spent several weeks there and we got accustomed to the food. From there we went to Austria, where we have family. We have family here in America and we moved here nine months after we arrived in Austria.

Roddy: Would you say that your experience has helped you to be a stronger person?

Houman: Once I investigated the Bahá'í Faith and understood its history, I understood the significance of the trip. When I read about the early days of the Bahá'í Faith, when Bahá'ís were persecuted and martyred, when the 20,000 Bábís – the early followers – were martyred to initiate the Bahá'í era, the significance kicked in a little more. There was a spiritual significance to it instead of just an escape from the country because we were in trouble.

Roddy: It seems absurd to many people that you would be killed for your faith or be asked to give it up. Why do you think, even 150 years ago when the Bahá'í Faith started, there was so much persecution?

Houman: It is a question of authority and power for governmental officials and leaders. When they feel that someone is coming in and changing the lifestyle and traditions, it is a threat. Also, at the beginning of every dispensation there is natural opposition. That opposition is what Bahá'u'lláh talks about in the Fire Tablet. He says, 'Were it not for the cold, how would the heat of Thy words prevail, O Expounder of the worlds?'[10]

Roddy: Can you explain that? What does that mean?

Houman: I think the heat and cold refer to the conditions of life. When a person is going through struggles and tests, it seems extremely cold, like complete despair. That's when the words of Bahá'u'lláh, or of any Manifestation of God, shine most. When the Bábís were persecuted in Iran, such that 20,000 of them were martyred for their faith, that seems like coldness to me. It makes the heat of Bahá'u'lláh's words much more powerful because these people sacrificed their lives. Other people are confused and caught up in leadership, power, authority and money. These people sacrificed their lives for a spiritual cause.

Roddy: So could you look to the histories of other faiths, like Christianity, and see similar kinds of opposition?

Houman: A lot of people questioned Christ's faith. They said, 'Where's He from, He's not supposed to be from this particular place. I don't believe Him.' Then they persecuted Him because of where He was from or the way He looked. Muḥammad was also confronted with religious persecution.

Roddy: They made Muḥammad flee from His own city, Mecca, to Medina.

Houman: Moses was also persecuted in the early days of the revelation of His teachings. As human beings we have to acknowledge the history evident in each of the dispensations. Still now, in Iran, there are persecutions.

Roddy: When you came to America, you were in a new country with a new language. What was it like growing up in this new environment?

Houman: I fell into the trends of the American lifestyle, the patterns of American society. I wasn't deep into the Bahá'í Faith; I didn't

have any source of guidance within myself. I heard the principles around me – the oneness of humanity and racial unity, for
instance – but I didn't have the guiding source within me.

Roddy: You hadn't discovered those for yourself; you just heard them
through the mouths of other people?

Houman: I just followed what the rest of the people were doing. I was
like, 'Yes, this is fun, so I'm going to do it. Yes, I feel loved, so I'm
going to do it.' But it wasn't real love; I just went with everyday
things with no purposeful approach to life. In my junior or senior
year in high school, my sister suggested I say some prayers and
she gave me a prayer book. I started saying prayers and then I
started going to Bahá'í functions with other youth. With my other
friends I would play football or basketball or go to parties. It was
a completely different scene with the Bahá'í youth – there was a
greater amount of trust. I could definitely sense something, even
though at the time I couldn't describe it.

Roddy: Was there a struggle, like a tug of war, over which direction
to go?

Houman: Yes, that was a hard struggle and it's ongoing. When I
started hanging out with new people, my other friends would call
me and say, 'What's going on, how come you're not coming out
with us? Why are you conforming to something?' There was a
lot of curiosity. I didn't want to say, 'Parties are stupid, you guys
shouldn't be drinking.' It wasn't about forcing my views on other
people. It was about going with a natural trend in my life.

Roddy: Even though you were born into a Bahá'í family and you went
through a profound experience as a child, you grew up here and
discovered what you believe in your heart. You had to go through
your own experiences and struggles to reach that realization
yourself.

Houman: It's an ongoing thing; it wasn't a one-time discovery. A
common point of confusion for people learning about the Bahá'í
Faith is thinking that to be a Bahá'í you have to be completely
educated and live out every single principle of the religion but

that's not true. If that were the case, I wouldn't be able to join the religion. Back then, I was dealing with different issues. In my group of friends, racism would always come up. I was completely blind to it back then but I see what it is now. Back then, we would play some sport and our group was so ignorant that when playing with people of other races, we made racial and ethnic comments that were obviously picked up from other kids in the group or from their parents. I had no idea what those names meant. If I said to myself, 'I'm not perfect in the department of racial unity, so I can't become a Bahá'í,' then I wouldn't be able to realize my mistakes. The Bahá'í Faith is not about being perfect and then jumping into it.

Roddy: If two people are both trying to be good, why will one call himself a Bahá'í while someone else will not?

Houman: One reason is faith. It's understanding what this world is all about. My purpose on this earth is to develop myself spiritually. 'Abdu'l-Bahá said that the purpose of human creation is to develop ourselves spiritually. He compares our development to the child growing in the womb of the mother, the child developing his arms, legs and eyes in order to function in this physical world. In a similar sense, I'm trying to do exactly that same thing by following the Manifestation of God for this day, Bahá'u'lláh: following His principles and trying to develop those spiritual arms, legs and eyes. For example, I'm learning humility before God and love for God's creatures on earth, along with principles such as love, submissiveness and general brotherhood and sisterhood.

Roddy: If there are all these different Manifestations of God, why do you choose to follow the teachings of Bahá'u'lláh?

Houman: It's been prophesied in other religions that this Prophet was going to come. The principles Bahá'u'lláh taught, such as racial unity and the equality of men and women – when you actually put them into practice, they stand out. When you're involved with the principles, they make sense. These things made my heart want to join this Faith and be involved in a process in which I'm helping others, giving a solution to others, being involved in discussions and struggles with others, in order to realize these principles.

Roddy: So on one level, it just feels like this is right. On another level, Bahá'u'lláh's principles and teachings directly relate to the state of the world today.

Houman: Exactly. There's also trust and faith. I might die soon, or not so soon, but why take the risk of going astray and following the way everything else is going right now when there's eternity waiting for me?

Roddy: What problem are you working on in particular?

Houman: Race and the equality of men and women are two issues I've learned a lot more about recently. I'm becoming more aware of situations where racism is completely clear or very subtle. Situations where the equality of men and women is just completely not there. Those are the two key things that are directly involved in my life right now.

Roddy: In our society, there are fundamental problems. You probably have an awareness of certain obstacles and challenges that young people are dealing with.

Houman: Carrying out the principle of the equality of men and women, associating with other males, seeing the treatment of women in particular – I can't describe this in a couple of sentences. It's elaborate but in general it's a pain that men have to feel. I won't say every single man because we're all different but men can't be so scared that they turn and walk away and get caught up in the male ego, which is so subtle sometimes that we don't realize it's there. We have to be willing to accept the pain that's going on. I can think of examples. I'm not saying I've dealt with this in the right way necessarily but I've learned from it. A couple years ago, I went on trips with the Bahá'í Youth Workshop – we do dances, dramatic pieces and performances about the principles of the Bahá'í Faith, such as racial unity, ending violence, the equality of men and women, diversity and things like that. On our trips the issue of the equality of men and women came up. It was often completely painful because I personally didn't understand what was going on. I think it's time for men to feel the pain that women have been feeling for so many years, the oppression even within daily conversations – the complete dominance of men. There are misunderstandings. A lot of men refuse to accept that women are developing characteristics that have been set aside for so many years. It's a pattern we get caught into. I know I get caught up in it all the time, following old patterns of behavior. Especially as males, we are peer-pressured by other males into having that macho style, that dominant, in-control thing, not letting in, being careful not to be submissive to a woman. That atmosphere defines society right now. 'Abdu'l-Bahá talked about mental alertness, intuition and the spiritual qualities of love and service that women have.

Roddy: Would you say that men also have those qualities?

Houman: I think men have those qualities but women, when given a chance to develop them, are stronger than men in those areas. Males and females have two different complementary purposes. We have to develop our own individual roles on this earth. Women bear children and men should complement that process, for example, in a marriage. There are stereotypical roles for males and females now. For example, women staying at home and cleaning the house, doing the dishes, taking care of the children or doing the laundry and the men going out to do the work and coming back home. Those are some behaviors we have to understand and change if necessary. If the family finds, through consultation and unity, that some of those behaviors are the best way for them to be, then fine, but in general I think they've been oppressive and have held back progress. Change requires an attitude of humility, submissiveness to another source – which is God – and also consultation under all conditions. A person should always trust his or her inner feelings, thereby being true to the self. When we feel that something is wrong or something is right, we can go with that feeling.

24

The Merest Atom

Charity Pabst

On those occasions when I can let go of myself and my attachment to things I have to do and be, occasions when I slow down and see what's in front of me, I feel so humbled. Humbled because I get a clearer perspective of what I am in relation to everything around me.

When I am at the ocean, I have this sense most clearly. There I am, sitting on these gigantic rocks looking out on what seems to be an infinite expanse of blue. Enormous waves roll in and crash against the ledges in front of me. Suddenly I realize how powerless I am in the face of this mighty water, how easily I could be overcome and swept away by it. I sit there in awe, transfixed by the beauty and power of this place and I think, my God! This beach, this ocean in front of me, is AMAZING. Yet what I see is just a fraction of the whole ocean and the ocean is just part of the large body of water that covers our planet. Our planet, which seems so huge, is just one of many in this solar system. I am so blown away because I can't even begin to conceive of the limitless space beyond and around us and our sun. Whew.

One can easily be overcome by the majesty of the ocean and the immeasurable expanse of the universe but what about those smaller, seemingly insignificant things? Consider insects, for instance. There are thousands of species of insects crawling and flying around on this planet. These billions of creatures are specialized for specific tasks and suited to live in different environments and each has its own role to play in the natural life of our world. And flowers – how many types of flowers are there? Thousands? Millions? Flowers of every shape and size and color and fragrance, flowers suited for various climates, providing sustenance for creatures of all kinds, flowers holding the keys to cures for diseases and aiding in the healing of our bodies.

And the body! Now that's another thing entirely! I think about the sheer magnificence of the human body: organs, bones, muscles, respiratory and nervous systems, our brain, our blood vessels and veins; all of these parts work together to run our human 'machines', whole works enclosed within our skin, shielded and protected from everything outside. That's just our bodies, our temporary vehicle in this world, the throne of our inner temples. Each of us has a soul – a spiritual nature that mirrors, to a degree, the attributes of God.

If I stop and think about anything in this world, there is no end to my amazement. How much greater is my amazement when I think about the fact that God created all of this and that we are His creation. Bahá'u'lláh talks about how God called creation into being:

> Behold, how immeasurably exalted is the Lord your God above all created things! Witness the majesty of His sovereignty, His ascendancy, and supreme power. If the things which have been created by Him – magnified be His glory – and ordained to be the manifestations of His names and attributes, stand, by virtue of the grace with which they have been endowed, exalted beyond all proximity and remoteness, how much loftier must be that Divine Essence that hath called them into being?[11]

God didn't sit and toil in a great heavenly workshop trying to figure out how to make 'creation'. He simply called everything into being. If that in itself is not the most amazing thing, I don't know what is.

If I can't even conceive of the size of the universe or the magnificence of the animal kingdom or the variety of plant life or grasp the nature of the human soul, how can I imagine the greatness of God, who created it all? The answer seems clear: I cannot. All I can hope for is an ever-increasing astonishment with what I see and know, remembering that each and every created thing is a sign of God. This kind of seeing is a way to come closer to God. Looking for the signs of God all around me is one way to know and love a part of that 'Divine Essence'.

25

Rod on God

An Interview with Roddy Khadem by Lila Rice Marshall

Lila: What image comes to your mind when you think about God? Do you have any visual images or any idea of what you picture when you talk about God?

Roddy: I think of more than one thing. I'm aware of all the people I've ever met, especially all the great people and all the people who have a lot of spirit and love that they shine forth. So they come to my mind when I think about God. But that's more what I associate with God. Also what comes to my mind is a picture of nature and the world, atoms and planets. I picture Manifestations of God in their human form. But I'm always very keenly aware that these are just shadows of God. If you add them all up, they're not God. Bahá'u'lláh wrote,

> Whatever is in the heavens and whatever is on the earth is a direct evidence of the revelation within it of the attributes and names of God, inasmuch as within every atom are enshrined the signs that bear eloquent testimony to the revelation of that Most Great Light . . . but for the potency of that revelation, no being could ever exist.[12]

So it's clear that if you look with your inner eye at anything in the world of creation, you can see the attributes and names of God.

Lila: To pin down one specific image is really impossible. I think often of people who are particularly shining or radiant. Then I have a lot of funny little images. Did you ever see *The Never Ending Story*?

Roddy: Yeah. Rad movie.

Lila: At the very end, the child empress has one grain of sand from Fantasia and it beams. This is like God inside everyone's hearts, this molecule of divinity that's inside everyone.

Roddy: That's rad! That's beautiful. It's true. And there's a paradox. If you look at a grain of sand or a small thing in life that seems insignificant, whether it's an atom or an action, it can seem meaningless to us. And that's a shame because that's the secret to meaning in life – these small things. The power of the divine exists. Bahá'u'lláh said, 'How resplendent the luminaries of knowledge that shine in an atom'[13] and He talked about how in a single atom there is the potential to become a sun. He said, '. . . how vast the oceans of wisdom that surge within a drop!'[14] That makes me think of the grain of sand.

Lila: Like you were saying, in the atom and everyday things there are such mysteries and power.

Roddy: It's a matter of looking into things with a searching eye. Everything can become a door to the divine, right? Every little thing. This is very much connected to what I was saying before about looking to little things. God is, in His essence, absolutely unknowable, absolutely unfathomable. Although God is unknowable in His essence, His attributes, qualities and names are in all of His creation. You can look at the different things in this world of creation – in the mineral kingdom, the plant kingdom, the animal kingdom – and you can find these names and attributes of God. We're not left totally clueless as to what this unknowable God is because we have all of these things around us to look to for insights.

Bahá'u'lláh said that humankind on this earth has a very special station because in each of the other kingdoms – the plant, the animal, the mineral – there are only certain names and attributes of God; there are limitations. Bahá'u'lláh wrote that in humans 'are potentially revealed all the attributes and names of God to a degree that no other created being hath excelled or surpassed . . . Even as He hath said: "Man is My mystery, and I am his Mystery." '[15]

This brings to my mind the metaphor of the mirror. The more we cleanse the mirror of our hearts from the dust and dross and dirt of the world, the frustrations of day-to-day life, the disenchantment with society and letting society get you down – the more we cleanse this mirror of the heart, the more we shine forth these names and attributes of God. It's like we're facing the sun. The sun is God and we are, essentially, a mirror. We have the potential to be completely clear and shine forth these attributes.

Hundreds of years ago there were some Sufi mystics who were really into this idea. One of them cried out, 'I AM GOD.' And the people around him said, 'WHAT? You're God? That's blasphemy!' And they killed him. But what he meant, it seems to me, was 'I have reached a state of such self-effacement, I have completely rid myself of all my attachments and my ego, I have completely cleansed this mirror, that now I'm shining forth God!' But this is a really important distinction. Although we have the potential to reach the station of mirroring the names and attributes of God, this does not mean that we're elevated to a high rank when we do. It is precisely at that moment that we are in the utmost state of servitude, of nothingness. There is no self anymore; we are absolutely humbled. So God is there and we are nothing more than a reflection. We are all limited to the station of man and are not capable of reaching the station of God or of a Manifestation of God.

From my understanding of the Bahá'í writings, the Manifestations of God were the only human beings who were perfect mirrors. Therefore, they were perfect representations of these attributes and names. But still, Bahá'u'lláh Himself said that even He had no knowledge of the Unknowable Essence of God. He said that! But from a human being's point of view, like you and me, if we want to know about God, the most we can ever comprehend is this realm of the names and attributes of God. The most we can do is look to the Manifestations of God. You know, it's kind of silly to categorize God but if it helps us to understand some of these differences that we find everywhere, then maybe it's useful. But I think that with all of this in mind, we need to be aware that God is absolutely unknowable.

Lila: And what recourse have we?

Roddy: Right. When you talk about these things they get really confusing! I'm just making an attempt to put it into words. When I talk to my friends and they say, 'I believe in God' or 'I don't believe in God' – their viewpoints are valid to me because it's important to look beyond the words that people say. There's a difference between the spoken words and what someone is truly saying. I have a good friend who says, 'I'm an atheist. I don't believe in God.' When I talk to him a little bit more and I have him explain what he's said, it's clear that what he's saying is, 'I don't believe in this notion of some old, bearded man up in the sky who points His finger at people and does these funky, magical things and zaps people with lightning.'

Lila: I don't believe in that either, so there you go.

Roddy: And if that's the definition of being an atheist, then I am also an atheist. The words don't matter. This friend of mine believes in certain things. He doesn't call them God but he believes in certain ideals and principles as a matter of faith. All human beings, I think, have to believe in some things as a matter of faith.

Lila: It's part of being human! It also took me a long time to attribute my beliefs to what I now call God. It's the same thing but I think it's just the label that people have such a hard time with.

Roddy: It's an uncomfortable label. I find myself very uncomfortable sometimes using the word 'God' if I want to put a label on the things I have faith in. We all have faith in a lot of things. But to use the word 'God' you need courage. In the world right now, that word 'God' has so many negative connotations. I think it's perfectly understandable that people don't want to use it.

Lila: Where did those negative connotations come from? I don't understand. I grew up with them but I don't know why I had them. Those negative reactions are really interesting to me.

Roddy: I know that for a lot of my friends it comes from the fact that religions have become corrupt. Some religious leaders use their power to take advantage of people. Religion has become the cause of hate and enmity, so God is associated with that and religion becomes a joke or something evil. Those Sufis, back in the old days, felt in their hearts that God was so unattainable and so out of reach that even to use the word 'God' was too direct a connection. They thought it was blasphemy. So they would simply say 'the Who'. It was their meager attempt, a very admirable attempt, to make God that much more separate.

Lila: Do you personally think God to be more of a 'Who' than a 'What'?

Roddy: I personally think that God is a 'Who'. When you're on a treasure hunt, there are little hints along the road that point you in the right direction. These to me are like the signs of God, attributes like love, compassion, justice, patience and knowledge. These are all the signs that point to 'Who' is.

Lila: A treasure hunt! But on this treasure hunt you never actually find the treasure.

Roddy: But you can be happy just finding the little signs. It's really exciting when you find the clues, right?

Lila: Sometimes it feels silly to call God anything! It does seem kind of ridiculous. This is a quote from Daniel Martin, a Catholic priest from New York: 'The word "God" comes from the Anglo-Saxons. It means "One who is greeted".' So God is a greeting, a recognition of that mystery in the atom, in a person, in a grain of sand.

Roddy: That's beautiful. We can experience that feeling when we're happy or when we feel love for another person. You know those little hints that you find along the road, right? That's probably what it's all about, that's when we're shining forth that light.

Lila: Yeah. When we're seeing and recognizing. It's good!

Roddy: We shouldn't think that God is separate from us and that therefore we don't have to worry about what we do. I think the whole point of these insights is to become gradually closer to God. Our love and our knowledge of other people and our desire to do good, to be happy and bring about happiness – that is really being close to God. So you can think of God as unknowable but that doesn't mean that you can't be close to Him. The most important thing is living happy, productive lives and trying to work on ourselves, our virtues, our qualities; to make a change, to touch the lives of others.

Lila: It's not about ideology, it's about love!

Roddy: Exactly. Sometimes talking about these ideas can help us to put things together. It's about our day-to-day lives. I heard somewhere that it's better for a person to be a good carpenter than to know all of the holy scriptures and words of God from all eternity because knowledge without action is useless. We really have to keep that in mind. For spiritual growth, it's actions and deeds that matter, not words, forget words. 'Let deeds, not words, be your adorning.'[16]

26

My Life as a Camera

Joshua Homnick

Communications media, technology and dreams. It's completely and totally insane: the fact that I can send images and sounds, my own messages and information, anywhere in the world, almost instantaneously. And who am I? Nobody. I have no royal blood. I hold no high position in government. I'm far from the power of wealth. I'm just your average plebe.

Unbelievable. This is something the richest, most powerful emperors, kings, queens and religious leaders could never do just over a century ago (unless they possessed supernatural powers). I also have access to images, sounds, information and knowledge that the most adventurous explorers and conquerors couldn't even imagine.

One thing that strikes me about this technology is the way it warps the limitations of time and space – the way it distorts socio-cultural barriers. Let's say I call a pizza parlor to order a pizza: 'You want extra cheese?' Are his parents proud of this kid or do they even care? What dreamscape does this person roam in his sleep? I don't know this person, yet in a weird way his mouth is close to my ear and my mouth is close to his ear. It is like being cheek to cheek with a total stranger.

Try walking straight up to a stranger on the street – stand in front of him, really, really close. My guess is you'll immediately feel a tension. Next, put your cheek next to his and tell him you'd like extra cheese on your pizza. Better yet, walk into a pizza parlor, go behind the counter and stand cheek-to-cheek with the pizza person. What happens?

Here's another thing about the time/space factor. Back in '92, at the Bahá'í World Congress in New York City, I worked on the international broadcast of the four-day event. Something like 30,000 Bahá'ís attended the Congress. People from hundreds of countries gathered together to commemorate the centenary of the passing of Bahá'u'lláh. A showing of world unity and oneness like this was never before witnessed. Grass roots people came together from every cultural background, happy, lots of cheek-to-cheek. If you thought world peace could never happen, standing in the middle of that crowd, the question was: how could it not happen?

There was so much going on over that four-day period, being everywhere at once would have been ideal. Let me tell you, I know, because I was everywhere, thanks to video technology and the longest sleepless stretch I've ever experienced. We were all so sleepy, I remember my cameraman falling asleep behind the camera. I ended up having to do a lot of my own shooting.

The production team literally took over a whole hallway of rooms at the Hilton hotel. That hall became the Bahá'í World Congress TV grand production central. We set up something like five high-end video editing suites, computer graphic consoles in closets, audio booths in bathrooms . . . it was great. My job was to do the segment of the international satellite broadcast on the youth activities and to help out with anything else I could. This gave me open access to everything and anything – behind, under and over the scenes.

But this isn't what I'm talking about when I say 'everywhere at once'. What I'm talking about is that hallway in the Hilton. That was everywhere at once. Sure, I spent a few hours a day out in the field but I spent most of my time in and out of editing sessions, looking through miles of footage. I saw everything that happened from at least three different angles at once. Suddenly I had more sets of eyes than I'd ever want. The whole situation was so unreal, it was like being in a dream state. I went to events, experienced them in person, felt the presence of it all and interacted with all the people but time and space were turned on their heads when I walked down that hall in the Hilton.

One more point about working on the TV broadcast of the Bahá'í World Congress: the thrill of finding friends of mine who I hadn't seen in years in other people's footage – and consequently searching them out at the gatherings – added an extra dimension to the whole notion of having multiple eyes.

This connects with something 'Abdu'l-Bahá said with regard to the soul and dreams:

> . . . in sleep, in the twinkling of an eye, he traverses the East and West. For the spirit travels in two different ways: without means, which is spiritual traveling; and with means, which is material traveling: as birds which fly, and those which are carried.[17]

I immediately relate this to the power of movies and television – not the content but what the medium allows us to do, the way it messes with our sense of space and time. I can show you a scenic shot of Papua New Guinea and immediately cut to a scenic shot of New York City. Or I can show you the same scenes from multiple perspectives at the same time – like a dream, like 'spiritual travel'.

Start paying attention to how close you get to people over the course of your average day. When I say close, I'm talking distance. How often can you see the pores and little peach fuzz hairs on a person's face? How many times during the day are you close enough to count a person's individual eyelashes? Calculate how much time you spend with people on a daily basis. How much time do you spend with each person? Figure out whose thoughts and character you know the best. Who are the people you spend the most time with? Who are the people you get the closest look at? Who are the people you know well? Try tracking down the source of what you talk about and think about every day and the information you exchange with people.

Compare your findings to how close the camera brings you to people in movies and on television, how much time you spend watching these people, what you know of their thoughts and character.

What's the point of this exercise? Pondering these questions led me to a deeper understanding of the power of the communications media, its celebrities and the fans who care so much about them that they shell out billions of dollars, worldwide, buying magazines and tabloids to find out what the celebrities are up to. People continually consume information and knowledge like this. I don't think that my relationship with the people who allow me to gaze into their faces for long stretches of time, who tell me their secrets and daily happenings, would be the same unless they felt I cared about them or had some sort of love for them. More importantly, if they didn't care about me or love me in any way, they probably wouldn't bother wasting time with me. I think the way television and film bring us into people's lives sends us a subconscious signal that these people love us and care about us.

If you go to a small city in the northern desert of Peru, or almost any city in South America, you'll find shantytowns sprawled out around it. Actually, they're more like cardboard villages, entire communities of squatters. The oddest thing is that besides the national flag flying high over many of the cardboard shelters (they believe raising the flag will make them less likely to be kicked off the land), large TV antennae protrude in every direction. It's surreal.

I didn't have a television in my house until I was 15 or 16. The only reason we got one was because I won it on a television contest broadcast nationally in Chile. The contest just so happened to be a break dance competition and the television exposure led to appearances on all kinds of shows and commercials, which led to more of the same. Eventually the break dance fad died out but I was still asked to be in commercials. About five years later I went back down to Chile for a visit and dropped in to see one of my old high school friends. My friend's maid came to the door (my friend's rich but not that rich – it's not hard to afford a maid in South America; the extremes of wealth and poverty are galaxies apart). Anyway, the maid looked at me really hard and then all of a sudden she exclaimed, '¡Oye, Vo' eri' el Chinto en la tele!' That's Spanish pronounced with a Chilean twist for, 'Hey, you're the little Chinese guy on television!' I guess I looked at her kind of funny because then she said, 'El break'n, el break'n!' She continued, 'The television makes you look Chinese, so my daughter called you "El Chinto".' She got this endearing look on her face and stepped closer: 'My daughter prays for you every day.' Now that freaked me out. Her daughter, living in some Santiago slum, with about .5 per cent of the opportunity and privilege I have purely because I'm white, male, American and . . . she's praying for me? She doesn't even know me! We've never even crossed paths! It's so one-way. What a weird, weird thing television is.

Soon after that I found myself on the Apache reservation in southern New Mexico, where I had spent a few of my infant years. This time, though, I was equipped with a professional TV camera and the opportunity to use the medium to benefit a small community where I could get to know who I was dealing with on a personal level. I worked with a tribe on a community-based project. The tribe's concern was that their youth were losing touch with their culture and ways and were forgetting their language. The youth seemed to have little self-esteem and they were way into alcohol and drugs. There were a lot of complicating factors involved, one of them being the mass media.

The tribe felt that the kids would rather watch TV than listen to the elders. They wanted me to use the medium the kids would pay attention to in order to motivate them. I made sure I had some extra cameras I could give to the kids, to do some of their own filming. The end result was what the tribal elders had hoped for but the resulting programs unexpectedly showed that the kids, as a collective, knew a lot more and were more concerned about things than the elders had thought. What I liked most about it was that it was a two-way thing. It was a thrill to use the medium to facilitate communication in a small community of people.

Something interesting I learned by doing the Apache project had to do with their old ceremonial dances. Back when the Apaches roamed the Southwest freely and had to defend their land from the white invaders and conquistadors, the war dance would psych them up for battle. The war chief would stand there with the drummers and singers and call out to the warriors dancing around in front of everyone, 'What are you going to do to the enemy?' The warriors acted out what they would do. This made me think of something I heard about ski racers who are successful because they visualize a course and go through the motions immediately before a race.

From this I eventually arrived at the notion that many people's attitudes toward interracial relationships are negative. They could never imagine, or envision, having a relationship with a person of another race or culture. But sit them down in front of a movie that includes the story of a successful interracial relationship, showing a couple overcoming obstacles, tests and difficulties, and those same people who wouldn't know where to start to think about an interracial relationship now have a point of reference. They can visualize it.

Everything I do is influenced by what I know or don't know. What I don't know could change everything I do know. Anything I do, every choice I make is influenced by information in one way or another and affects my perception of other information. Look up the butterfly wing effect in chaos theory – it has to do with the interconnectedness of everything. And now, even though I have a tendency to simplify things, I have no excuse: if I want to, I can ride the long trains of thought between science and religion, one religion and another, one cultural mentality and another. We can unravel the intricate connections uniting everything with everything: dreamlike abstractions, where the most absurd logic makes perfect sense. Our minds are capable of grasping and our tools are capable of delivering.

27

Into the Light

An Interview with Leili Towfigh by Heather Brandon

Leili Towfigh was 25 at the time of this interview and lived in West Medford, Massachusetts. She worked for ComTel Productions, Inc. in Marlboro, Massachusetts, and was also the co-coordinator of the Boston Bahá'í Youth Workshop. Leili has a degree in religion and intercultural studies from Bryn Mawr College. She is interested in multimedia technology as a way of disseminating Bahá'í principles in action. I spoke with her in a telephone interview to explore her outlook on media.

Heather: What's your job right now?

Leili: I work at a visual information systems company. We use the organization of information to get jobs done. That extends to public relations work, video documentation of construction sites, graphics and marketing. My boss, who is a Bahá'í, believes that your business is blessed if you do service as part of your mandate. As part of our regular duties every day, we have several service projects for various institutions and organizations.

Heather: What is some of the service work you do?

Leili: We're doing a documentary on a high school in Greenville, South Carolina, called *A Bootstrap for Generations*. The teachers there are very highly-educated African-Americans who were not hired by universities and colleges because they are black. Many people with PhDs end up teaching at this high school. They turn out incredible students, among them Jesse Jackson. We've interviewed people from the 1930s on. Also, we just finished a documentary for the government on African-American soldiers in World War II, which is intense. It's so cool. You might have heard in the news that several black soldiers were recently awarded the Medal of Honor for their valor in World War II but all but one have died. So they never got it. In the documentary, the soldiers talk about how in their own country they were being lynched, attacked and treated lower than animals and yet they begged to go to Europe and 'liberate' it. Many African-American soldiers were instrumental in liberating the Nazi concentration camps in Europe. The African-Americans' desire and yearning to serve their country by 'liberating' Europe is ironic because the Europeans originally enslaved Africans and brought them to the United States.

Heather: Tell me about your work in visual communications and multimedia.

Leili: We're working on a multimedia interactive kiosk on traffic safety for teenagers. Traffic accidents are the leading cause of death among teenagers between the ages of 12 and 18. The kiosk is used as an educational tool in schools. It includes video, music, words and clips from famous films involving traffic safety. It's very effective because nothing else is getting through to teenagers; it's a totally new thing, drawing on all of their senses.

Heather: Is your goal mainly to educate or are you also asking for feedback to improve the kiosk?

Leili: It's a pilot test. We educate the group but I also administer tests and feedback forms to the kids. They make a lot of suggestions. For instance, crash test dummies. The kids say it's stupid to show dummies that never die when they have accidents; they make kids think that they're invincible. The kids said to use more of the Australian-made films because they are hyper-realistic. The Australians actually went around with cameras in ambulances, waited for an accident to happen and filmed it. They're the most effective public service announcements I've ever seen.

Heather: The kids feel totally ready to see that?

Leili: Yes. The people in Australia did market research and found that kids are not swayed by death; they are swayed by dismemberment and disfigurement. Most of them don't care if they die but they care if they have to live a difficult life. One spot the Australians did shows two girls on a Saturday night, speeding down the road. They see some male friends. The guys start chasing them and the girls say, 'Oh, he's a babe,' and they look to the side for a second, laughing and giggling – boom! They smash into a car. It's gruesome. I don't know how they filmed it. Then the next thing you see is the guys rolling up and the girls screaming. One of the guys runs over to the other car. You hear a baby crying. The guy goes to the woman driving, he lifts up her arm and it just falls back down. Her eyes are staring at him and he says, 'She's dead, we just killed somebody, she's dead!' You hear the baby crying. The kids who saw this, their jaws just dropped open and they said, 'It gave me an idea of how many lives I would affect if I were reckless.' The crash test dummies don't do that.

Heather: I know you've done film and video work for various purposes. What are the reasons you love working with video? What have you learned working with the technology?

Leili: I like to use it as a tool. If something better comes along, I'll use that. I don't have that much prowess with it but it suits my purposes.

Heather: How so?

Leili: For example, when I went with a delegation of Bahá'í youth to the Fourth International Conference on Women, the United Nations conference in Beijing, we couldn't bring our whole ensemble [the Boston Bahá'í Youth Workshop] to present our model of development. We went there to present a workshop to international development workers on the role of young men in raising the status of women and the importance of partnership between men and women. We couldn't get that across with the handful of people we could afford to send, so we brought a video to capture the fragrance of that process. Seeing is believing and if you see respect between young men and young women, you know it's real. It's much more effective than saying, 'No, really, they respect each other and are dignified!' The video was a means of bringing that fragrance of hope and positiveness to a room of about 200 people from all over the world. Also, I met you through a film we were working on, called *Where's the Arboretum?* about race relations at Haverford College. In a project like that, where people work together to get a message across, message-driven or content-driven media can be a transforming process for the people involved in it.

Heather: Do you remember being in the film club together, working on a couple things?

Leili: Yes! Like the film *Water-Ink-Light* that we made.

Heather: What made you want to make a film about ink?

Leili: Why? I think it looked good. The whole light and color thing is content-driven. Starting in the mid-1800s, there were great advances in technology, science, music and art. A lot of paintings at the time were infused with light, as opposed to the ash-can school and the dark grungy thing that was happening before that. At the time, the whole world, every atom of the planet, was affected by the coming of the Báb and Bahá'u'lláh. Whether we're aware of it or not, all of us are affected. Visual things, as little and insignificant as they may be, that try to communicate or glorify the light that has infused the world can be good and can affect people's hearts and put them in a more spiritual frame of mind. Our water-ink-light film can have an unconscious spiritualizing effect on someone's heart. It comes from a desire to glorify light in every sense of the word.

Heather: What is that spiritualizing effect?

Leili: Well, it has to do with a whole aesthetic. It can be hard for people to maintain a spiritual outlook. In North America, with racism, materialism and moral laxity constantly clawing at our heels and dragging us into the pits of mire in ways that we're 90 per cent of the time not even aware of, we need to have a spiritual environment and a pleasing atmosphere. That can simply mean refusing to have the things one looks at be as mired in the mud as the things around us. So making a short film about a Japanese bowl of water and brightly colored drops of ink falling onto a clean white page and spreading out with water – that is saying something about how one's atmosphere can be bright and colorful rather than muddy. The content of any work of media – writing, drawing or video – should match the form. There should be an inner harmony between those two, to affect the heart.

Heather: The next step, along those lines, is to affect the mind, once you affect the heart with the way something is presented.

Leili: That's a cool way of putting it. That relates to what the Bahá'í writings say about education. The heart has to be attracted to a message. You can pile somebody's arms full of Bahá'í books and it doesn't mean they'll get something from them if there's not an attraction. It's like working with youth. There are many things on the minds of youth – violence in the home, dating culture at school, where there's constant intrigue and distraction from learning; abuse, rape, racism everywhere all the time. It's no wonder facts taught at school don't stick in people's brains. Education is about hearts connecting so that, as you say, the minds can then connect. It's impossible for minds to connect with one another on their own. They have to make that detour to the heart first.

Heather: Maybe it's not so much of a detour.

Leili: Yeah, maybe that's actually the highway that God has constructed for us. But instead we consistently use a broken-down little burnt-out bridge bicycle route, which doesn't even work and there's a huge traffic jam and people are honking at each other and having crashes.

Heather: Right. And traffic signs are pointing us in contradictory directions.

Leili: Exactly. If you want proof that minds alone can't connect, just take racism in North America as an example. You can legislate that everybody has to be integrated and you can have debates on Oprah and you can have the skinheads and the Al Sharptons fight but it has not changed a single heart. In their hearts, they are still hating. It's often a language thing. You're just changing language and the heart remains exactly the way it was before because there's no spiritual incentive to see how wonderful it is when our hearts connect. I'm not against the mind. I'm just saying it has to be part of that spiritual Interstate system that God has so beautifully planned for us.

Heather: That relates to the crash test dummies – they're a mental exercise.

Leili: The Bahá'í writings say that every soul is given a particular capacity at birth, be it a thimbleful or a bucketful, and it's really not for us to compare our capacity to that of others but instead to make sure our capacity is used completely by the time our short lives are ended. It has been said that God loves those who work in groups and I think that media can be a tool to help the potential of a group to come out. I witnessed that when you organized your multimedia workshop. You gathered a lot of geeky computer friends and geeky art friends and threw us all in a room and said, 'Work it out! You might think the goal of this is to make a multimedia piece that we can be proud of but really the goal is to practice the art of consultation, with so many diverse elements.' It was a challenge in a million ways – there were male-female challenges, there were techno vs. non-techno challenges, there were aesthetic vs. non-aesthetic challenges. We struggled through them but we had an incentive, such that we didn't dwell on personal problems and we made something. It was awesome. I've never experienced anything like it. To me, that's a wonderful use of the technology that the Bábí and Bahá'í revelations brought to the world for us. The purpose of technology is not to noodle around and be a nerd or whatever. I believe the purpose of this technology is to be a tool to unify humankind. The media, when used for the purpose of consultation and unity, brings out talent that one might not know is present. The more talent is brought out in service to humanity, the faster we're going to get world unity.

Heather: You've been such a pioneer in the projects that you've been working on that I trust you know about this stuff firsthand. You've taught yourself how to do things because your objective is right there in front of you. You don't revel in the technology.

Leili: Exactly. I compare some of the stuff I've been given an opportunity to do with media or with youth to various parts of my official schooling. I had a lackluster approach to some aspects of my education. I'd say, 'Ho hum, when's it going to be over?' I compare that to the joy and excitement with which I approach my work now because, again, there's that incentive of unity and connection with other people. If I can infuse that into my self-education and into my formal education, that'll be a great thing.

Heather: What about educating others with the tools that you've learned? Is that another aspect of what you want to do?

Leili: Definitely. A new definition of education came when Bahá'u'lláh's Revelation affected every living thing on the planet. I think it has to do with what Bahá'u'lláh taught about how this is the day in which every soul must see through his or her own eyes and not through the eyes others. That has a direct bearing on education. The new definition of teaching does not involve filling people full of facts. Instead, education should inspire and excite people to embark on their journey of independent investigation. I'm excited about that and that's what I can bring as a teacher.

28

My Dream, My Spirit, My Journey

Sarah Remignanti

This past summer, as I was trying to decide whether or not I should spend the year in Brazil, I had a dream. In it, I was alone in the semi-darkness on one side of a tall, thick wall built with stones that appeared strong and solid. When I looked above me, over the top of the wall, I could catch glimpses of a ladder that continued upwards towards the sky until it became lost in an impenetrable brightness that surrounded it. I was drawn to what I saw. My desire to climb the ladder overwhelmed me. I noticed the only way to get there was through an opening that had been made in the stones near my feet. I got down on my hands and knees to look and found that the opening was smaller than I had hoped. I would fit but the passage wouldn't be easy. I knew that once I began, the broken stones would scrape my arms and tear my clothes and that my hands would be buried in the dirt on the other side as I crawled through.

Now that I am here in Brazil, trying to find a place in a culture that is not mine and is unlike everything that is familiar to me, I remember my dream. It reminds me, always, that the difficulties I have as I leave my home to serve the Bahá'í Faith will ultimately bring me a peace that I've never known before. Already, after only a month, I've found that in sacrificing my personal comforts and facing difficult changes, I am filled with a love for the Faith that is so intense, I become frustrated at how limited I am and how hard it is to put the feeling into words. The Faith is a light so beautiful, so full of truth, that once you find yourself surrounded by it, you never want to be without it. And suddenly the tests you endured in your search for it become insignificant.

I decided to take a year off college mostly out of a need for something more than I had – a spiritual solidity of which I'd lost sight. My first two years of college were a good experience in many ways. I lived away from home for the first time, I found some incredible friendships and I took interesting classes. At the same time, it was difficult for me to discover the balance in my life that offered me the steadiness I craved. It was so easy to become caught up in everything that was happening around me. The more I tried to hold onto some priorities, the more vague they became. After a while I forgot what I should value as important compared to what actually was. Despite the positive advantages of being at college, I felt a lingering emptiness and a longing to fill it with something. By the end of my second year I realized that taking some time off to serve the Bahá'ís in another country would help me tremendously. I knew that reestablishing lost connections with the Faith and a sincere devotion to service would bring me the clarity I needed.

So here I am, helping to teach the third grade at an international elementary school in Brasilia. The school caters to the small percentage of the Brazilian upper-class and many of the children's parents work in the government embassies or as foreign diplomats. The children themselves are a challenge. They reflect their upper-class lives and have opportunities and advantages that few children in Brazil have. They are so used to having, asking and getting that it keeps them from developing an awareness of their limits as children in a school environment. They lack respect for rules, for their teachers and for their peers. At the same time, they possess a wonderful combination of qualities. They are the most affectionate, loving children I have ever spent time with and they are full of talent and energy that only need to be directed.

On the weekends, I help teach Bahá'í children's classes in a community called Samambaia, which is a *favela* (shantytown) surrounding Brasilia. It's such a contrast to spend the week with children whose lives afford them everything and to spend Sundays working with children who have nothing. The poverty in the *favelas* is unlike anything I have ever seen or could have imagined. It is so widespread that sometimes I feel helpless standing in the middle of such desolation. Children walk in the streets begging for food for their families, babies have babies and parents abandon their children every day. Sometimes it's so difficult to feel like you are helping at all because everywhere you look there's something else that needs attention.

Spending time with the kids of Samambaia is amazing. About 40 children, both Bahá'í and non-Bahá'í, show up for every class. After the difficulties I encounter with the kids at the international school, I welcome my time with the children in the *favelas*. Because they have so little, they appreciate everything. They are unbelievably respectful and helpful and they are so receptive to learning. They don't know what it's like to have and it's kept them from being jaded.

The first time I went to Samambaia, I helped pass out food, collected at the international school, to the poorest families. I was standing near the trunk of our car where we had bags of rice, beans and canned food. I turned around to see a little boy who looked about four years old watching us. He had a beautiful, sweet dirty face, shorts so ripped they barely covered him and bare feet. One of the girls standing nearby spoke to us about him in Portuguese. Later when it was translated, I learned that the boy's mother sends him out every day to ask people for food that he can take home to his family. All I could offer him was a large bag of rice and he turned away to go home. As I watched him walk away down the dirt road, I thought of the only four-year-olds I've ever known, spending their time playing in grassy backyards and memorizing *The Lion King*.

Working with the people in this community is an overwhelming experience. It keeps my life in perspective. I really look forward to my time there because the people are so sincere and spiritually receptive. They have nothing material to hold on to, so they are waiting for something greater – a spiritual comfort that will help them find meaning in their suffering.

I've really struggled with the work that I do here. I wonder why I'm spending so much time at the international school where they have two teachers for every 23 students, when the 16-year-olds of Samambaia have a first and second grade reading level. I find I have to remind myself often that I do have an important job. I am helping to teach the next generation of adults who are going to have government positions. These are the children who in 20 years will have the authority and power to change their country. Whether or not I understand it, the kids at the international school are probably always going to have the upper hand. So it's our job to teach them compassion, equality and justice. It's important to take advantage of that and extend their sights beyond themselves and their own social class. Then they will, hopefully, grow into adults who have a vision of their entire country and its role in world unity. And they will be willing to push for change where it is desperately needed.

The country itself is divided into very distinct classes. The lower classes don't have educational opportunities, which means they never get well-paid jobs, so they end up as maids in upper-class households where they are paid what I consider an inhumane amount of money for incredibly hard work. Nearly every middle- to upper-class family here has a maid who usually lives in the house with them and does everything from making the beds to doing the laundry. It is so much a part of life here that everyone assures me I will adjust to it. I won't. I will never get used to the idea that this woman spends endless hours in the kitchen making my food and doing my laundry for three dollars a day.

The language barrier has been a true test of patience for me. The only words I knew in Portuguese before I came were 'thank you'. I knew that it would be a huge obstacle but it is definitely the largest and most frustrating. I've temporarily lost my independence. Just last week I learned how to go to the store to buy shampoo and mail a letter at the post office by myself. I never thought about how vital communication is to everyday living until I found myself without the ability.

The people of Brazil are incredible. They are unceasingly kind, affectionate and patient. It seems that life for them moves more slowly and the easy pace leaves them happy and content. They take their time, they dance in the streets, they hug each other, they enjoy moments, they celebrate everything. In the US sometimes we are so caught up in living our lives for tomorrow that we forget today. The music and the dance of Brazil are true symbols of its history and remind me of a web stretched over the land, connecting every single person in the celebration of their country. On the whole, the people, the customs and the arts come together to give Brazil its own rhythm – a very slow, intense drumbeat that can be felt everywhere.

29

Sing Out My Love

Isisanne Prichard

As I set out to write this piece, I am bombarded with thoughts of the infinite definitions of prayer and the differing ways people go about praising the Unknowable Essence, which some call God, others call Allah, some call Goddess and thousands don't call anything. I could tell you what the books say, I could tell you what she said and he said and they said, and even what He has said but I have decided to tell you about my experience so that maybe one of you among the many who read this might be comforted by my story.

Prayer is the foundation of my spiritual well-being, the one thing that has the power to keep it all in order. It is the balancing factor in a world of chaos and clutter that keeps me focused. When I lose sight of that, I see it in my relationships, my sleep patterns, my speech, my everything-you-can-think-of related to a human being.

Last year I spent eight months in Bolivia. Although it is one of the poorest countries in South America, Bolivia is rich in the finest of gems: the gems of purity of heart and spirit, hospitality and unconditional love. My entire time there could be translated into a novel with all that I have to say about it but I will tell you simply of an experience that pertains directly to the topic at hand: prayer.

I went to Bolivia because the Bahá'í Faith is the most important thing in my life and all I could think to do was to share its beautiful message with others. Friends of mine were going to Bolivia and I thought, 'Why not? I have no other plans and what could be better than spreading happiness throughout the world?' This was the most exciting and frightening decision I had ever made. New culture, new people and new responsibilities: I had to open my mouth at whatever time it was deemed right to teach and I had to learn about the Bahá'í Faith. With a team of youth on a hillside in the Andes, I took whatever God gave me.

While I was in South America I was sent into the forest of the Amazon for a Bahá'í institute on group consultation. One of our assignments while stationed in Amborro was to pray and meditate individually from 6:00 to 7:30 in the morning. This may sound simple and routine to some but when you are sharing a small room with six other people – there were nine people on the team in total – personal space and time are very limited. We were asked to memorize prayers and writings so that we could be like soldiers in God's army, armed with the power of words, which are stronger than guns and weapons. I have always had trouble memorizing the Bahá'í writings. However, when given the task with time dedicated to doing so, I found that I enjoyed it and improved my ability to memorize.

On the morning of the second day, after bread and tea for breakfast, we broke into our individual groups – one team member and God – and set out for our special spots hidden in the forest. Equipped with a prayer book, a clear mind and a heavy chair for sitting, I trudged through the dew-laden grass and the twisted flowering trees until I found a clearing with a perfect view of the sun rising over the peaks of the mountains which poked through the low-flying clouds. Butterflies of colors and designs only nature could have created danced before me, creating an almost surreal world for my most incredible hour and a half yet.

I sat down in my chair and watched the world as it lay in front of me, untouched, undisturbed and indescribably beautiful. I couldn't decide what to do first – to pray from the book or from my heart; to meditate and reflect in silence or to sing out my love – a million things could have been done in this most precious time and strangely I decided to just be and hoped that I had made the right decision.

As I sat and concentrated on my breathing, I felt light and alive with an energy that I had never felt before. I started to recite my favorite prayer, one I had recently memorized and which has very special meaning for me. I said each word as if it were my own. I asked with sincerity and analyzed every word as it left my lips. As the tears of complete joy started to stream from my eyes, my voice became shaky and I started whispering without meaning to lower my voice. My prayer did not waver and my tears did not cease but grew stronger. I felt as though the only part of my body that was still moving consciously, aware of its physical reality, was my mouth, shedding sweet words into the atmosphere. I did not close my eyes to concentrate and I stood knee-deep in yellow flowers, the world and I as one and at peace.

It was then that I finally gave in to the All-Knowing. I realized that I could not hide anything from God, that He indeed knew everything about the world, the universe and me and that all the hiding of my imperfections was, in the end, to no avail. With that release, I truly felt free in every sense of the word. Free from the world, free from myself, free to do anything, free with myself and free with God.

As I stood there, I felt the weight of me come back and the petty goings-on of the world infected my mind once again. The only difference was that I felt able to wipe away all of that stuff and clear the slate whenever I needed to.

In all the 19 years of my life I had never prayed like that. I haven't felt such absolute peace since. I now realize that it is all a process. That old saying rings true: practice makes perfect. It applies to everything, spiritual and physical.

Now I know that I don't need the Amazon at my front door or even another country, person, place or thing. All I need is the knowledge of God and my soul to be in tune and this feeling can return to me when I am ready. It is not easy. I thank God for the bounties that have been bestowed upon me, for the fact that I can commune with Him through the most exhilarating, spirit-filling, smile-making, tear-jerking lines of sweetness and love that have yet been revealed to this planet.

Now when I stretch to the sun in the morning and kiss the stars at night, I roll the words in my mind and off my tongue to let the breeze carry them sweetly to the ears of the rest of the world – in the hope that others, too, may find solace in my prayer.

30

Recite Ye the Verses

An Interview with Mojgan Sami by Kalím Armstrong

At the time of this interview Mojgan Sami was 26 and residing in Haifa, Israel, doing volunteer service at the Bahá'í World Centre. She has had a pretty interesting life. At the age of 17 she traveled around India, Japan and Hong Kong. She graduated with honors from high school and college. Mojgan attended Lewis and Clark College in Oregon where she studied International Law and Middle Eastern Studies. She backpacked across Europe for six months after graduating from college, and then came back to Bellingham, Washington to find a job. She ended up working as a journalist for a television station and she wrote and acted in commercials for an advertising agency. When she was interviewed Mojgan had just finished a two-year Master's degree program at Johns Hopkins University, one year of which was earned from study in Bologna, Italy. She is a very bright, talented and knowledgeable woman.

Kalím: You have been traveling since you were 17. Where have you traveled and what was your motivation?

Mojgan: Actually, I've been traveling since I was born. My parents love to travel – it's hereditary. I have traveled to Asia, Europe, North America and Africa. But I've been traveling in the sense of 'independent travel' since the age of 16. My motivations stemmed from whatever event I was traveling to, usually a Bahá'í conference or dedication of a Bahá'í temple. I don't look at traveling as a form of vacation. Traveling teaches you to see with your own eyes and hear with your own ears. The world is your classroom and the people are your professors.

Kalím: How have your travels helped to shape your identity?

Mojgan: Before I traveled I considered myself American or Persian depending on my mood. After I started traveling I started thinking of myself as a Bahá'í. I began to understand that Bahá'u'lláh's world order is truly for every single human being, not for just a select few. Bahá'u'lláh wrote, 'It is not for him to pride himself who loveth his own country, but rather for him who loveth the whole world. The earth is but one country, and mankind its citizens.'[18] Traveling led to my desire to serve the Faith in an international setting. When I say serving in an 'international setting' I mean serving the institutions that work for the progress of humanity through education and awareness – institutions that work for social and economic development, human rights and so forth. This is why I studied international relations and specialized in economics and international law. I wanted to understand the world environment in order to apply Bahá'í principles.

Kalím: You must have had some difficult situations in your travels. Can you think of an instance where prayer helped you get through a sticky situation?

Mojgan: Once I was traveling with three other youth from Strasbourg, France, to the Czech Republic. We had just attended a Bahá'í youth conference. The car trip went smoothly until we hit the border of the Czech Republic and were delayed because of typical customs stuff. By the time we found a youth hostel, it was midnight. Youth hostels close around 9:30 at night. We had nowhere to go – the Bahá'í Center was closed and we couldn't find anyone. So we all said a prayer. All of a sudden, a group of about five Czech students – not Bahá'ís – came toward the hostel and stared at us. One of them asked in English, 'Where you from?' We replied, 'America, Luxembourg and France.' The Czech students were in awe. Mind you, this was the first year or so that Eastern Europe had seen any Westerners! They were so excited to meet us. One of them asked, 'Where you stay?' We told him the hostel was closed and asked if he knew of another place we could stay. He said, 'We have two rooms, we give girls one room and boys one room. You stay in our rooms.' Not only did the wonderful students give us their rooms but they offered us food – apples, which are very difficult to find in Eastern Europe! – and they wouldn't let us pay them for anything. They kept saying, 'You're our guest, you're our guest.' Not only did prayer help us out of a difficult situation but it taught me a lot about generosity and kindness.

Kalím: Are attitudes about prayer different in the countries you have traveled through?

Mojgan: Good question. In Asia I noticed that prayer and meditation are mixed. They are not separated. In Europe people pray in churches. In the Middle East and here in Haifa, everyone prays differently – in churches, mosques, synagogues. Bahá'u'lláh has changed the way people should pray. For example, the Bahá'í obligatory prayers are meant to be said in private and are between you and God, whereas the Muslim obligatory prayer can be said in public and people say them no matter where they are. Also, being close to the Bahá'í shrines here, I notice how important the 'pre-prayer' attitude is. Why do you think all the Bahá'í shrines have beautiful gardens around them? To prepare us for entering a sacred spot and offering our prayers to the Beloved. No other religion in the world takes you through a spiritual journey before entering a place of prayer. This has taught me that no matter where I am, I need time to prepare and detach myself from worldly concerns and vain imaginings in order to pray to God.

Kalím: What does prayer mean to you? Why pray?

Mojgan: We should thank God every day for allowing us the bounty of asking for His assistance. What other form of creation can supplicate its Creator? Can a chair ask the carpenter for guidance? Can an animal? No. Humanity has been given the distinct honor of being allowed to pray to God. This is an amazing thing to think about. So prayer is a bounty. Prayer is also a way to seek guidance and offer praise and gratitude.

An interesting aspect of the Bahá'í view of prayer is that you could be praying and not even know it. Work done in the spirit of service is considered worship. So if you are working and your intention is service, whether service to your boss, your editor, your teacher or humanity at large, then you are worshipping God! 'Abdu'l-Bahá stated, 'The man who makes a piece of notepaper to the best of his ability, conscientiously, concentrating all his forces on perfecting it, is giving praise to God.'[19]

Bahá'u'lláh states in a Hidden Word that He has given us the earth and everything in it – the only thing that He has kept for Himself is the human heart. However, the only way we can feel the love of God is to purify our hearts. This can only be done through prayer and service. Shoghi Effendi wrote to an individual believer in 1936, 'It is not sufficient for a believer merely to accept and observe the teachings. He should, in addition, cultivate the sense of spirituality which he can acquire chiefly by the means of prayer.'[20] After all, the goal of the Bahá'í Faith is the development of the individual and society through the acquisition of spiritual virtues. How else can you acquire such things if not with prayer?

Kalím: Can you give an explanation of how prayer and meditation are different?

Mojgan: I love to walk in the Bahá'í gardens surrounding the shrines here in Haifa and read holy scriptures or meditate on a particular passage. The gardens are so peaceful, calm and beautiful. They help me become detached from all my problems and concentrate on the Bahá'í writings. Bahá'ís don't have a particular method of meditating. How you meditate is up to you. Every individual must find his own level of communion with God. Bahá'u'lláh asks us to pray and fast from the age of 15, the age of maturity.

You asked me earlier whether I think praying is a chore. If you love someone, do you want to make him happy? Would it be a chore for you to make him happy? If we want to show our love for God, we must fulfill His commands. Praying is one of those commands. It's interesting to note that Bahá'u'lláh also asks us not to pray TOO MUCH! In the Kitáb-i-Aqdas Bahá'u'lláh states, 'Read ye the sacred verses in such measure that ye be not overcome by languor and despondency. Lay not upon your souls that which will weary them and weigh them down, but rather what will lighten and uplift them, so that they may soar on the wings of the Divine verses towards the Dawning-place of His manifest signs . . .'[21]

Kalím: What are the Bahá'í obligatory prayers and what is their purpose?

Mojgan: They are specific prayers revealed by Bahá'u'lláh the recitation of which is binding on Bahá'ís from the age of maturity. We can choose among three different ones and recite them in private. Sometimes I think of praying as something we do for ourselves because we are usually asking for something from God, asking for assistance, guidance and so on. However, reciting our obligatory prayers is something we can do for God because we are acknowledging our humble state in comparison to God's power and might.

Kalím: Do you think youth should go to college before doing a year of service?

Mojgan: I have asked myself this question a million times. I've read that one should ask the question, 'Will my education assist me in serving the Cause?' Personally, I thought my education was necessary to my serving the Cause. So I got a Master's degree before applying for my year of service. But you know what? The service I'm involved in here at the Bahá'í World Centre has nothing to do with my studies. This doesn't mean that I studied for nothing. What it's taught me is that serving the Cause has nothing to do with how we want to serve it but, rather, it has to do with how the Cause needs to be served. If you are dealing with this question, you have to pray and pray for guidance. Another thought: who says you can't serve and study at the same time? Of course, there is a balance in all things. Shoghi Effendi, in a letter written on his behalf, stated that a 'good Bahá'í' is 'one who so arranges his life as to devote time both to his material needs and also to the service of the Cause'.[22]

Kalím: What kind of work are you doing at the Bahá'í World Centre?

Mojgan: It would best be described as a photo historian. I am assisting the Audio-Visual Department in the identification and cataloguing of historical photographs. It's the most amazing job in the world. The history of the Bahá'í Faith comes to life in front of my eyes and affords me the opportunity to study the life of early believers.

Kalím: Where and what did you study?

Mojgan: I did my undergraduate degree at Lewis and Clark College in Portland, Oregon, where I majored in International Relations and minored in Middle Eastern Studies. My graduate degree was at Johns Hopkins University School of Advanced International Studies. Since I wanted to learn about the world system and international economics, I chose International Relations and International Economics as my areas of concentration. It is important to study the Bahá'í writings but one should also study the prevailing non-Bahá'í intellectual theories in order to learn to convey the Bahá'í ideas so others will understand them.

Kalím: Why did you decide to study Middle Eastern Studies?

Mojgan: Mainly to study the region of the world which was first impacted by the coming of Bahá'u'lláh.

Kalím: Living at the Bahá'í World Centre, surrounded by people who are serving the Cause of Bahá'u'lláh, an environment where prayer is daily sustenance for all, how is the vibe different? Can you feel the power of prayer and see its results?

Mojgan: Actually, I was talking to my friends about this. There is a 'vibe' here, as you call it, that is unexplainable. No matter what you think of, it happens. It's not because we're praying for something in the Holy Land that it happens; it's because being in the Holy Land, we pray for the right things. So they happen. Does that make sense? Bahá'u'lláh says to know thyself. Serving in the Holy Land makes me very aware of my actions and duties to God, so I begin to know myself. And as I know myself better and better, I realize that there are things I need to work on – patience, humility, kindness. So I pray for those things and then I'm tested. If I want patience, I get tested until I develop patience. Tests are a part of prayer.

31

Of Earth and Structure

An Interview with Della Fallah by Erika Hastings

Della Fallah, 22 years old at the time of this interview, was
a student at the University of Victoria in Canada. She was
majoring in Art History and planned to study architecture after her
graduation. After a long day of college, Della and I wandered into an
empty room near her husband's wing of campus – engineering. The
buildings were new and modern and as we walked by them, Della
said to me, 'I used to walk by buildings and not pay any attention
to them. Now I can't pass one without analyzing every detail of it. I
think buildings should jump out and grab you, grab your attention.'

Erika: What is it about the field of architecture that appeals to you?

Della: I'd like to concentrate on vernacular architecture – houses and
personal homes. For me, architecture is the design and it has a
great influence on our surroundings. That's what interests me. To
be able to influence people, the way they think and live their lives,
changing their minds, is kind of cool. Creating a message through
architectural design is what I really like about it.

Erika: What inspiration and changes would you like to produce, since
you're going to be focusing on the home?

Della: I'd like to make the home more organic – make it more a part
of its natural surroundings and bring nature within the home.
In the designs I've done, every house has a garden in it. I think
when people are working in the city, they want to come home and
I think having nature in the home is very important. It brings
people closer to earth, realizing that they are a part of the earth,
not disassociated from it. It's not something that they experience only on a camping trip on the weekend. It's a part of their

everyday lives. One house I'm working on now has three interior gardens to make the house and the nature blend into one.

Erika: Are there other designs you have seen that illustrate this idea?

Della: A good designer who illustrates this is Frank Lloyd Wright, the American architect, in his early work. Also Gaudi from Barcelona, Spain, has strong natural components in his designs. There is an apartment complex of Gaudi's that really inspired me. It's very round, almost gushy looking, and just melts. In the interior there are two shafts that bring light into the homes. Recently I was in Dallas and a lot of big office buildings are being constructed there. That's given me many new ideas.

I also have my own drawing of a house. It was inspired by a Japanese house as well as by the work of Frank Lloyd Wright. Everything is vine-like. It has a center hall from which everything branches out. There are three or four interior gardens and everything is very accessible. The ceilings are high, which give it a sense of being outdoors and very open and airy. All the windows are straight and level with the ground so you can walk, or step down in some cases, right into a garden area. The outdoors is accessible from every single room in the house. You don't have to go somewhere else to go through a door to go outside. You're basically living there. You're just covered by the roof.

Erika: Is this your dream house?

Della: It's not necessarily my dream house – it's not very practical. But it illustrates the point of bringing nature and the house together. As for my dream house, I've always liked Spanish and Italian villas, the type with stucco and tiles. They are organic in that they usually have interior gardens and courtyards and you walk through nature to get into the house.

Erika: What influenced your interest in this type of design? It reminds me of Roman architecture.

Della: I first got inspired by Spanish and Italian villas where, like I said, you go through the garden in order to get to the main house. Also the work of Frank Lloyd Wright has inspired me – his way of designing a building – giving it a linear aspect and having a central focal point with regard to the design of the house.

Erika: What dreams do you have about applying your skills and what do you hope to add to the field?

Della: I want architecture to affect people in a positive way. Like I said, I want my designs to bring nature back to people so they learn to respect it. Even if I were to design public buildings, like offices or libraries, I would want to bring that whole idea in there, nature and man together. I'd like to bring in a more open, friendly atmosphere.

Erika: Can you talk a little more about how you see your architecture affecting people?

Della: I think certain buildings have different roles to play. For example, the Bahá'í structures on Mount Carmel, in Haifa, Israel, have a classical Roman and Greek architectural style which will last through the ages. They invoke a feeling of heritage and grandeur without being very ornate. If you look at the old cathedrals of Italy, they're very simple. And the Shrine of the Báb, with its golden dome – you can look at it and maybe not know what it is but you realize that it's something special.

Erika: Something holy or sacred?

Della: Yeah. You can see through the architecture that it is something very important. The Bahá'í Houses of Worship as well, especially the one in India, are very inviting but at the same time awe-inspiring. If these sacred places had been built in a Modernist or Cubist style, with very plain forms, then I don't think they would have had the same effect. I think the choice of architecture illustrates the importance and sacredness of the place.

Erika: What feeling would you like to invoke through your architecture?

Della: Not necessarily awe – I want to make people think about how they are a part of one planet and that they're really one of many. Or have them look at something I have designed and think, wow!

And then maybe lead on to something else. It's really kind of mystical . . .

Erika: Like how we're all interconnected?

Della: Yeah, everything's interconnected. That's what I'd like to show. It's hard to explain. I just want people to feel something when they look at my work, not just passively observe it. I want them to look at it, try to figure it out and come up with an understanding themselves.

Erika: How do you think humans and the environment are connected?

Della: Well, we are of the environment. If there were no air or water we wouldn't live, so I think it's stupid for us to deny that connection between ourselves and nature. We are very influenced by the environment around us – we are of the earth. We are born to this world and then our bodies return to the earth while our souls go on to another world. Our physical body is of this earth.

Erika: There is a quote from 'Abdu'l-Bahá about the home being a place of joy and delight:

> My home is the home of peace. My home is the home of joy and delight. My home is the home of laughter and exultation. Whosoever enters through the portals of this home, must go out with gladsome heart. This is the home of light; whosoever enters here must become illumined . . .[23]

What are your ideas on this concept? How do you think you could incorporate this in your architecture?

Della: I think a home can be inviting in the way it's decorated but more importantly, it's a reflection of the individual. A home can also be inviting by the way I am as a person. If I'm warm, kind and loving and invite people in, they will come and have a nice time. Structurally speaking, I can design a very inviting home but the person who is living there may not be warm or joyful, so no one will want to enter that home. You may go in and everything's

145

white and the host is only worried about getting stains on the carpet so you don't even want to sit down.

Erika: So what kind of challenges do you think you'll have in the field of architecture?

Della: Just entering the field of architecture as a woman! It is still very male-dominated. Also just getting into architecture school – that's a challenge! Just get me into architecture school and I'll be happy. Also I'll be challenged doing what I'd like to design. Maybe in the day time I'll work as a person who fills in doors in a plan and then do something else on the side. I haven't thought about that much actually – the challenges I'll face. I just want to do it and then face them as they come.

Erika: What influence do you think the presence and the domination of men has had on the field of architecture and on buildings around the world?

Della: Well, there are a lot of office buildings, for example, which are very masculine. They're upright and geometrically shaped.

Erika: Are there any female architects whose work you have studied?

Della: When you look at the history of architecture, everyone is male. There is no female influence, so that means the people who are studying architecture will continue on that same theme. If we had more female architects, even if we only introduced them into the art history classes, they could bring something different into the field of architecture – otherwise everyone's just copying what the dominant influence has been. The only female architect that I've heard of is a woman who designed the Vietnam War Memorial. It's sad that she's the only one I've heard of. There have to be more women out there doing things but we just don't study their work. Essentially, I think if you're a good architect, you're a good architect, regardless of gender. It's just that the avenues and opportunities are not as open to women.

Erika: There's such a wide diversity of cultures, tastes and building materials from all over the world. Does this play a role in your imagination?

Della: Like I said before, I look to the traditional homes of an area and the local ideas, like the Spanish and Italian villas. When I was in Japan, the traditional Japanese house influenced me. I look at the traditional vernacular architecture – not something that was duplicated from some other style but something that is very local. Then I take elements of them and put them together.

Erika: Who has influenced you in your decision to become an architect?

Della: I'd always thought that I wasn't smart enough to be an architect. I'm not very studious but I do have an imagination. My husband encouraged me to do it. He said, if you like it, do it. If you like it, you'll be good at it. Just go for it. Then I thought, yeah. If I like it, I'll be able to do it. Someone will like my work, someone in the world has to like my work. So I'll just do what I want.

Erika: What do you think is significant or exciting about a career that makes environments and living spaces for people?

Della: I think it's going back to the whole organic connection with the house and the ground and the earth being one.

Erika: What about your specific style of living?

Della: (laughs) You mean all the clothes on my floor?

Erika: The way we live in our spaces and how people are so attached to their own personal space, especially their homes.

Della: I've noticed that for many people with homes now, or even apartments, even collective living – their home is not a place that people really enjoy. It's a place just to live and to keep the rain off their heads. I think a home should be so much more. It should be a part of you. It reflects your mind set and what you do in life – if you have a very good living environment, it will be reflected in your actions. I just go home to sleep and eat and then I leave for college. I've made our home comfortable but I don't enjoy it, whereas I think you should go home and feel at home and relaxed.

32

Finding the Inner City

Kalim Armstrong

I remember the trees, the birds, the boundless acres of undisturbed nature. Oh, the joy of chopping wood for the fire on cold winter nights. Many days I spent walking through the woods with uninterrupted thought, walking for miles with no worries, no complications. Just me and mother earth.

About six months ago I moved from the small town of Durham, New Hampshire, to San Francisco, California. I thrust myself into a world populated by materialism and abounding racial discrimination, homelessness, drug abuse and seemingly infinite opportunity. I came to the city for several reasons, mainly to study photography and digital media.

A friend who came to visit from New Hampshire said this about the city: 'In the country you can scream as loud as you want and no one will hear you. In the city you can scream as loud as you want and no one will care.' It was funny at the time. But it's true. I tried it. Here in my new home, I see so many people without a common goal, without a conscious sense of unity.

I found many things difficult soon after moving to the city. Everywhere I looked I saw homeless families, drug addicts, prostitutes, trash and a lot of angry, unhappy human beings. At the other end of town I saw some of the most expensive homes occupied by some of the wealthiest families in America. How could anyone live surrounded by such imbalance?

We have been making homes for our families in villages and cities for thousands of years. Travel, until recently, was limited to foot, horse and carriage. Cities were centers of learning and culture, great places of worship and the homes of kings and queens. With the industrial revolution, the modern city emerged, based around business, materialism and decadence. The social systems were completely altered with the newly-found potential and power of the middle class. In the mid-1800s the world witnessed the beginning of modernism – the invention of the telegraph, photography, the automobile and the beginning of the contemporary city. At the same time, a revelation so powerful that it illuminated the whole earth arose in Persia – the Revelation of Bahá'u'lláh.

If the modern city emerged simultaneously with a spiritual new breath imbuing the earth, then why are the great cities, the great cultural, economic and religious centers also homes for the worst crimes and atrocities of which humanity is capable? Many people immigrated to the United States in search of a better life. Some found opportunity in the new world but many found broken dreams and great difficulty. As cities grew and could no longer accommodate the great surge of new residents, they devoured every inch of habitable land. As the cost of living increased, only people with money were able to afford housing. Without institutions in place to prevent this, the poor wound up in sub-standard housing, in development projects, low income housing, or worse, on the street.

'Abdu'l-Bahá explained the different natures of man – the animal and the spiritual. He said that the body is the physical, or animal, nature of man:

> When man allows the spirit, through his soul, to enlighten his understanding, then does he contain all Creation . . . But on the other hand, when man does not open his mind and heart to the blessing of the spirit, but turns his soul towards the material side, towards the bodily part of his nature, then is he fallen from his high place and becomes inferior to the inhabitants of the lower animal kingdom. In this case the man is in a sorry plight![24]

Such is the case with our cities today. They are based around corporate structures and banks. No longer is the place of worship – the church, the mosque, the synagogue – the center of life. The office and rituals of work have become the focus of life and money earned the goal of life. There are people hungry in the streets because our technology has surpassed our humanity. The sick state of civilization can only be remedied by a spiritual cure and not by welfare reform, tax cuts or food stamps.

In my old town when I walked home at night, the only thing I feared was that a monster might jump out of the woods and eat me. Now I'm afraid to go to the corner store because I might get robbed or shot. Where am I? What's going on? From the comfort of my home town I could talk about homelessness and drug problems and, in my matter-of-fact and inexperienced way, offer solutions. Now I walk down the street and see a young mother sitting on a corner covered with dirt, holding her baby and begging for change. Now I see a 15-year-old girl on the street corner selling her body to men old enough to be her father who drive fancy cars and dangle $100 bills in front of her face. Now I'm approached by someone late at night who thinks he's Elvis, asking for a quarter. I know if I give him any change he will probably spend it on alcohol or drugs. I see this every day and go to sleep at night in my warm, safe bed knowing that thousands of people are trying to sleep on the cold concrete, not knowing when or how they will eat their next meal.

Living in a big city requires a degree of hardness, like a shell. One thing I struggle with daily is not letting my new hard shell veil my humanity. It breaks my heart to see so many people suffering and yet giving someone a quarter will not eliminate poverty and hunger in America.

'O people of the world! Build ye houses of worship throughout the lands in the name of Him Who is the Lord of all religions.'[25] 'Say: The Mashriqu'l-Adhkár is each and every building which hath been erected in cities and villages for the celebration of My praise.'[26] What modern cities lack with all their skyscrapers, houses and streets is a center. Not a financial downtown or a city hall but a center that is a house of worship, a place for social services and for administration. This will be a shelter and medical center for the poor and a place for learning, a place where individuals with mental problems can receive aid and not roam the streets homeless. A house of worship, the center of every community, would bring together all its diverse inhabitants under one banner. Although not a new concept, it would be a step in the direction of a unified society.

The city and country are both wonderful places. Small towns and villages have a feeling of community and closeness that cannot be replicated in the city. Only in the country can you experience the earth as it might have been in the past. However, often, because of their isolation, small towns do not see diversity and remain locked into the cycle of prejudice.

The city, with all its problems, is also incredible. It is a testimony to history and what we as humans are capable of creating. Its architecture, bridges and subways are still a marvel. Only in the city can you encounter people from all walks of life, from every inch of the globe. To be in a city is to witness the coexistence of all humanity.

The world is in a state of confusion, a state of adolescence. We stand at the crossroads of a new age, confronted with what the future will hold. Where we make our homes affects our mental state and our outlook on the world. Still, life in Central Africa is not so different from life in New York City. We are all spiritual beings, growing and developing regardless of geographical location. It is undeniable that American cities, being trend-setters, have a unique opportunity to lead the world in spiritual progress – just as they have in material ways. Many people look at the city and see a polluted, over-populated, materialistic world. Only the rejuvenating power of Bahá'u'lláh's Revelation can transform the cities, the country and, in turn, the whole earth into what is destined: the home of a divine civilization.

33

God and Mom

Amelia Villagómez

If I had a penny for every time my mom told me, 'Stop watching television, and start your homework!' I'd probably own the house we live in by now. Throughout my entire life my mother always, and I mean always, stressed education. She reminded me that education was the difference between making it in life and not making it. She lectured me occasionally, saying, 'Either you work hard now and have it easier later, or you have it easy now and work hard later.'

I never understood her reasoning. Why did she have to stress education so much? What was the big deal? You go to school, you endure the boring lectures, the hurtful gossip, the constant nagging from teachers on how you are capable of more. So what? Maybe I won't be a doctor or a lawyer but I'll get by. Why do I need to learn the quadratic formula, the velocity of a F-16, how to diagram a predicate noun, the significance of the Declaration of Independence or the parts of a whale to be successful in life? Am I ever going to sit down and calculate the parabola of a basketball? When I jump on a plane to Houston, am I going to calculate the plane's velocity? Is anyone ever going to say, 'If you don't tell me the significance of the Declaration of Independence, I'm going to hurt you'? I don't think so.

For centuries people have survived without formal education and school, so why can't I? If I just learned how to harvest food, raise my future children and build shelter, I'd be okay, right?

By quickly looking through 'Abdu'l-Bahá's talks in *The Promulgation of Universal Peace*, I find the answers to my headful of questions. When He was in Philadelphia He said, 'When all mankind shall receive the same opportunity of education and the equality of men and women be realized, the foundations of war will be utterly destroyed.'[27] Wow! I guess education really is important – so important that it can bring an end to war. And when women are as equally educated as men, we will not send our children to war. I guess by learning about how costly wars have been in the past in terms of lives and money, we can learn that war is not productive and only destructive. I guess history class would be a bit useful then. But I'm still not convinced. What else is there?

When He was in Montreal 'Abdu'l-Bahá said:

> Bahá'u'lláh has announced that inasmuch as ignorance and lack of education are barriers of separation among mankind, all must receive training and instruction. Through this provision the lack of mutual understanding will be remedied and the unity of mankind furthered and advanced. Universal education is a universal law.[28]

Let's see, what else? At another talk in Montreal 'Abdu'l-Bahá said, 'Through the broadening spirit of education illiteracy will disappear, and misunderstandings due to ignorance will pass away.'[29] So if I can get a good education, I will be a part of world unity. The skills of reading and writing are quite important, then, to the success of the world. If we all learn how to communicate properly then we can get along a lot better. Maybe to speed up the process I could tutor someone or encourage an academically challenged person. I guess as an individual I can really do a lot.

Bahá'u'lláh wrote:

> Knowledge is as wings to man's life, and a ladder for his ascent. Its acquisition is incumbent upon everyone. The knowledge of such sciences, however, should be acquired as can profit the peoples of the earth, and not those which begin with words and end with words. Great indeed is the claim of scientists and craftsmen on the peoples of the world. Unto this beareth witness the Mother Book on the day of His return. Happy are those possessed of a hearing ear. In truth, knowledge is a veritable treasure for man, and a source of glory, of bounty, of joy, of exaltation, of cheer and gladness unto him.[30]

The Bahá'í writings tell us that we should not only be book-educated but also educated in virtues, religion and music. I now know why my parents emphasized a musical education for me. For seven years they forced me to play the piano but I never understood why. Bahá'u'lláh elevated the importance of music, saying, 'We, verily, have made music as a ladder for your souls, a means whereby they may be lifted up unto the realm on high . . .'[31] So this is why my parents did that – what a gift they bestowed upon me! And virtues . . . I'm reminded how important it is to express virtues in every aspect of our lives. No one wants to be treated like dirt, so regard everyone as gems – that is basically the purpose of all the virtues. My parents also told me that without religion one does not have guidance. So the Báb, Bahá'u'lláh, 'Abdu'l-Bahá and my mother all agree. I had better listen.

I think education is more than just what you learn in school. Let's look at the whole picture. At school, you usually don't leap straight from class to class. You usually linger outside and talk to friends. You learn the skills of communication and kindness and that is just the beginning. Friendship introduces all kinds of virtues. By being a friend you have to show kindness, love and compassion and you have to listen. So you learn virtues. This is beginning to tie in with what 'Abdu'l-Bahá said. Education expands into the fields of art, science, manners and communication. Other skills are necessary for survival, like consultation, a very useful and handy skill that will one day be used to create world peace.

One Bahá'í teaching is the independent investigation of truth. There are no clergy in the Bahá'í Faith and each individual is responsible for learning and understanding the Word of God. So I guess that although I may not need to diagram a sentence, I need a good grasp and understanding of the language to read the Word of God. That is where English class comes in handy. And the sciences – humankind can't advance without them. I'm reminded of another Bahá'í teaching, that science and religion must agree. Although I may not need to know the velocity of a F-16, such knowledge is crucial to improving and developing technology. Plus, in science I learn other things which are useful to society. For example, without technology and medicine many more people would become sick and die from things like the common cold or chicken pox. The world is expanding and growing and its people have to be educated or the planet will be off-balance. Now that makes sense!

I'll just take out the Bible, *Bahá'u'lláh and the New Era* and my geometry book and begin my journey striving to establish world peace. You know, all these years I've been told that I can't bring about world peace and that the whole idea is hopeless. Yet I can make a difference through education. I'm ready to break down those persistent walls of prejudice that have kept me separated from my true brothers and sisters. Won't you join the vanguard and be a part of the process?

34

Laboring Serenely

An Interview with Caren Rosenthal by Lila Rice Marshall

Caren Rosenthal, aged 29 at the time of this interview, is from Natick, outside of Boston. Just before I spoke to her she had spent several months studying and serving as a midwife at Maternidad la Luz in El Paso, Texas, a clinic in a border town between the US and Mexico.

Lila: You come from a Jewish family. How did you become a Bahá'í?

Caren: When I was 12, my family and I went as tourists to Israel. We were staying in Tel Aviv and took a bus ride one day to Haifa and visited the Bahá'í World Centre with its beautiful gardens. In the gardens, my sister and I were overwhelmed. We didn't know how to describe it at the time. We were deeply affected by what we saw and when I went back to start high school, there was a Bahá'í in my class and I started finding Bahá'í books. I found one in a restaurant, one in a subway.

Lila: You found one in a restaurant?

Caren: Yes. It was in one of those restaurants that front as libraries. I found a little white book, a prayer book with gold letters saying *Bahá'í Prayer Book*. All the places I went and traveled to in my life after that, I took that with me. I would display it – you know how you hang something up, just lean it up against the wall and look at it. I would try to read it sometimes. One time when something was really weighing on me, I decided, 'I'm going to memorize one of these prayers.' I copied it down and stuck it in my wallet. Even in college I had that prayer book. I would notice people, their behavior and ways of interacting, and I'd think, 'Wow, that's kind of an interesting person,' and then I'd find out that the person was a Bahá'í. That happened a number of times.

Lila: So are you the only Bahá'í in your family?

Caren: Yes. One night after I had become a Bahá'í I was sitting at home with my mother, grandfather and grandmother. My grandfather was about to have some surgery. Everyone was a little agitated. We decided to pray together. I got out a Jewish prayer book, the Qu'rán, a lot of Bahá'í prayer books, a Bible, and the Bhagavad Gita. Everyone could choose what they wanted. We sat together and prayed and everyone chose a Bahá'í prayer except me. My grandmother passed away last year, while I was studying here at the clinic. This may be a segue into talking about maternal and child health and midwifery because there is so much in the Bahá'í writings about the purpose of life here in this world, acquiring spiritual qualities in order to have the 'limbs and members' we need for the next world. We're provided with the metaphors of gestation and birth in the Bahá'í writings. Reflecting on the beauty of gestation, prenatal care and birth is very similar to reflecting on the majesty of being alive in this world, striving to know God and loving Him and being born into the realm of glory that's waiting for us.

Lila: Is that where your interest in midwifery came from? Or was that something you recognized later?

Caren: I served for two months at Hospital Bayan in Honduras. You asked about midwifery – this is what I wrote after the first birth I attended in Honduras:

> I saw my first newly-born baby on Saturday. I did not see the birth. I had been with the mother throughout the hours of her labor, walking around inside the hospital and talking with her aunt and mother, with the staff. When she actually gave birth, I was tending to another child. But I saw the Honduran doctor who was doing his internship there deliver the placenta and I saw the baby, who had on its tiny shirt, put on with Pat's help. Pat was the nurse. A sense of overwhelming wonder about what it must be like to leave the womb and enter the world. I noticed particularly her hands, shriveled,

reptilian, long fingernails, moving vigorously, holding tightly to my fingers, so, so small.

What does it mean to be such a tiny, noble being? Filled with rich gems to be mined throughout one's life. I watched her try and succeed eventually to open her eyes, to see what she might discover about the world she had entered from the womb of her mother. The light was too strong for her tiny eyes so used to darkness and she could not open them for long. She drew her hands up over her eyes. I was overwhelmed with love for humanity that had its basis on a common sense of wonder, not that we all suffer but rather that we are all born noble, with unimaginable potentialities.

It's more than suffering that we share. Why not concentrate on the pure and sanctified nobility and greatness of us all? We are only developing babies, all of us in this world, clinging to the hem of God's love and protection and great mercy. How can we ever be so ungrateful as to harbor any animosity whatsoever, or even become angry with each other? We are all God's dependent helpers of babies. Why don't I live like I know this?

So I decided that I wanted to study babies.

Lila: So that was when you decided?

Caren: I had been working in the field of maternal and child health; I had been doing things with Bahá'í youth; I had been doing things about societal violence and domestic violence. It was important to me to figure out how to perform a craft rather than simply work with words. I wanted to add this component to my education. I'm in the middle of finishing a Master's in Public Health. My thesis is about the programs, interventions and policy changes that grew out of the 1985 Third World Conference on Women in Nairobi. More specifically, I'm looking at a document on forward-looking strategies for the advancement of women that emerged from that conference and projects around the world that evolved out of that document concerning the role of family and societal violence in development. There was a document published by UNICEF called *Battered Dreams* about the human and economic costs of violence in international development. I'm looking at the role violence plays systemically and in the family and how that influences setting up maternal and child health projects. There are aspects of human rights law, considering women's rights as human rights.

Lila: Are you able to incorporate your work in Texas into your thesis?

Caren: Yes. What I've done here assists me to understand the clinical aspects of prenatal care and birth, as I look at different projects around the world, the documentation of those projects and the legislation that various countries adopted based on the Nairobi document. I want to emphasize that I came to do this training for seven months as a part of getting my Master's. It was important for me to study and work in a resource-constrained environment where I could really use my hands and learn skills. This will assist me to be understanding, compassionate and knowledgeable in another way, giving me more capacity to interact with more people.

Lila: That is the role of an educator.

Caren: Yes. 'Assessing', 'determining','analyzing' – these concepts are associated with writing my thesis. But I want to add 'listening carefully to somebody in another language', 'explaining things' and 'being patient with the questions people ask about the changes in their families'. Do you see what I'm saying? It's a different way of educating myself and therefore it makes me a person who can, in turn, educate others.

Lila: Have you attended a lot of births?

Caren: Yes, since I been here I've been to more than 50 births, maybe 65, and that was all in the course of seven months. We work 24-hour shifts almost every other day.

Lila: You shared with me the extract from your journal, which was a beautiful description of that first birth, but you said that you didn't attend that birth itself. Actually seeing a birth – what's that like?

Caren: There was one birth last year at Naw-Rúz, the Bahá'í new year. I thought this was a very special experience, a baby being born on the eve of Naw-Rúz, 20 March.

This woman had been in labor for a long time. She was in and out all day. She was walking around but her labor started picking up late at night. The head was born first, just as the sun was coming up. There was just a tiny little ray of light on the first day of the new year. There was this perfect little baby. The head came out and restituted, which means that it moved – the head was born sideways but it turned up so the shoulders could come out. This little baby's eyes opened right away – right away. And that's something that I have watched in all the births – the eyes. Some babies kept their eyes closed; some – fewer – open their eyes right away. But this one, on this very first day of the new year, with this one ray of light coming in the window, opened her eyes and blinked a few times and looked around before her body was out. It was so extraordinary and so sweet and such a reminder of the fact that we are all in that position.

We are in a womb-like state at this point. The Bahá'í writings use metaphors like the birth of a new world order or the fact that we go through tempests and trials in order to reach a better state. That metaphor vividly illustrates what it's like to watch babies being born. The Universal House of Justice asks us to labor serenely. The more I watch labor and births and realize the concerns they evoke – how much emotion, how much sound, how much noise – things that may seem, to an unskilled eye, like despair – the more I see them as a way of preparation. These are a physical body's response to something that needs to happen. The degree to which you can labor serenely really has a bearing on the outcome.

Lila: Having a tranquil heart.

Caren: Yeah, exactly. To see that particular baby, on that particular day, with those wide eyes open – that was the essence of infinite serenity. If mothers are the first educators of children, there is such a huge responsibility to become unselfish, serene and capable.

Lila: What about hospital births versus home births?

Caren: Midwifery in the United States is separate from obstetrics and gynaecology and even from nursing. There's a tendency to think about direct-entry midwifery as non-medical, not effective or not sufficient to meet complications that could arise. It's really important to think of all the options that we have. Just as there's a diversity of temperaments in the way that we go about cultivating the spiritual qualities in this world. We know that there's only one Divine Physician. We're all simply physician's assistants; we are not the Divine Physician. I think it's important to consider the temperament and capacity of all the people involved and not to exclude from consideration any birthing method because they're all important and valid if they're considered with an open eye, an open mind and an open heart. There are different skills required for different circumstances. I don't go around saying, 'Everyone should have their baby with a midwife' or 'Everyone should have their baby in a hospital.'

Lila: Have you ever experienced problems with traditional obstetrics? It sounds like you have a wonderful understanding of it.

Caren: I have sometimes found that a lack of capacity to be open to different methods is coupled with a lack of capacity to be open to a diversity of temperaments and personalities. I have found myself in a kind of ambassadorial position. I have my feet in different places: I'm working on my Master's in Public Health, I'm doing midwifery and I also have the bounty of working with Bahá'í youth, which I think provides a framework for cultivating spiritual responses to the difficulties that come at us.

Lila: It seems like an open mind helps to open your heart.

Caren: Yes. Those things are really important to consider. The Guardian of the Bahá'í Faith talked about how only the spirit of a true Bahá'í can reconcile all these ostensibly opposite things, like justice and mercy. I think we're asked as Bahá'ís to strive with ideas that seem contradictory but which, if we open up to them, can be unified and create an alchemic change. A kind of alchemy happens when you hold different things together in your mind and you come out with something brand new that seems intuitive, that provides a vocabulary for people, something they're longing to say. Just like assisting someone in a birth, the task of the Bahá'í is to assist people to find a new path so they can turn around and say 'I did this myself' not 'you did this for me'. I think the way we share the Bahá'í writings is similar. How the writings will assist you to mine the gems of who you are is quite different from what they may do for me.

Lila: Is midwifery something you want to continue?

Caren: I am going to assist a midwife doing prenatal care. It's important to me to figure out how to incorporate some of the Bahá'í teachings into this work. I hope I will also attend some births as an assistant to this midwife.

Lila: It sounds like you have lots of goals. Are there other ideas you have for the future?

Caren: I'm very grateful to have had the opportunity to work and study at the clinic. I'd like to continue working with local, small-scale initiatives but also with national and international organizations. There are things happening in the nation and in the world that make the time ripe for realizing a vision of partnership between women and men, to see the family as a nation in miniature, for this vision to come to the fore and provide a new vocabulary. When I finish my Master's, I'd like to work with national or international agencies in the field of development. I'd like to focus on ways in which violence and the lack of consideration for the inherent nobility of women and the family impede progress in all settings. There's a lot of work to be done. We're told in the Bahá'í writings to get together with like-minded people, to use the art of consultation to bring new ideas to the foreground and not be held back by a paralyzing fear that prevents progress. I think the more we pray about what we are and what we can be, the more we're given the capacity to labor serenely.

35

Dear God

Mojan Sami

A couple of years ago I seemed to be missing something from my life. As I ran around in circles trying to find something to fill this void I was feeling, I lost something else: my faith in God. I slowly seemed to be retreating into the dark corner of every room and my happiness seemed to be caught beneath me, struggling, drowning and losing its pulse. I wanted to ask for help but I wasn't sure who to ask.

I finally had the courage to talk to someone about my sadness and the advice she gave me was prayer. She said that praying would probably be my only option at that point. But there was something discomforting about this. The thought of praying daily seemed so forced, so ritualistic. I had had the option of prayer all my life and now I needed a friend. The thought never crossed my mind that praying might take care of that.

Instead I grabbed my pen. I have always been a writer. When I was seven years old I wrote a book about a girl with no friends who had an emotional connection with a koala bear. When I was eight I wrote a book about four friends who camped across the world together. I still have these books but I rarely look at them. So much more writing has been done since that time.

But even as a child, I felt that I was writing for someone. I never intended to keep a record of my stories and poems and thoughts so that I could look back on them someday. Rather, I kept them because I thought that someone else would read them. But until that day when I took my pen and wrote between sobs and tears, I never knew who I might be writing for. This time it seemed clear.

I needed a friend. So when I took my journal and wanted to begin writing, I hesitated. I had spent all these years writing to myself. Disappointed, two words formed at the top of the page: 'Dear God.'

I hesitated to write any further. I believe that even when people write in their journals or diaries, they cloud the truth. There is so much permanence in writing something down, which makes it difficult to express our most arrogant, violent feelings on paper.

Instead we write songs or poetry – making us seem artistic rather than human. But I knew that once I wrote the words 'Dear God' there was no pretending. If I were to lie, God would know. There was no reason to make myself compassionate, unselfish, or humble because God knew what I was thinking. I was writing to someone who was watching me all the time. So I began:

May 31, 12:05 a.m.

Dear God,

It seems ages since I've communicated with You. I have felt that something has been missing from my life – now I wonder if it was You all along?

I know that my communication with You makes me feel more at peace with myself; I realize that it is You who calms the havoc and soothes the chaos. Unfortunately, I have been having difficulty confronting You. Usually it's because I feel worthless and embarrassed but sometimes it's to punish myself.

I used to dream about the things I wanted. Now I whisper back to myself about why I can't have them. 'I want a car' has become 'I don't deserve a car'. 'I want to fall in love' has become 'I don't deserve to fall in love'. 'I want to be happy' has become 'I don't deserve to be happy'. Maybe YOU could whisper something in my ear? Maybe you HAVE been whispering and I just haven't been listening! So maybe now it's time for You to shout.

No, my writing to God did not make me feel happy and refreshed instantly; it made me feel horrible. Who was I to exchange words with the Almighty? Who was I to believe that maybe, just maybe, He might be listening to me? My corner grew darker and deeper and I wished that I hadn't been so arrogant and childish as to believe that I could write to Him.

The next 24 hours were brutal. In an attempt to distract myself, I thought I would write something else. I opened my journal and stared at the blank page, hoping to dodge the inevitable. I couldn't. I began again, with the words 'Dear God' at the top. This took me somewhere new. I was writing like I had never written before. It was honest, pure and I made discoveries about myself as my pen moved rapidly across the page. It didn't faze me that my hand was tired – the only thing that mattered to me was that I was making a new friend and I didn't even have to impress Him. He knew I was human and that I would make mistakes. I felt Him on the other side of my words. 'Could it be?' I thought. 'Could it be that I might have an unconditional friendship? Is it possible that I might have a friend who has more faith in me than I do in myself?'

June 1 1:29 am

Dear God,

It's funny – sometimes I can hear You speaking to me. I don't always listen but it's only because You ask so much of me. But I hear every word, God. I'm sure You can hear me, my thoughts. You know all of my dreams (maybe You're the one sending them to me). I want to listen to You but it's not always that easy. And sometimes I wonder if I'm only hearing what I want to hear.

Okay, so I'm not a dedicated meditator. I don't always jump at the chance to pray for Your assistance. I'm afraid that if I ask You for help and don't follow Your advice then I will have let You down. So I stay quiet – within my own thoughts – so that I will only let myself down when I reach the point of failure.

You scare me. You scare me because I want so badly to do the 'right thing' for You and I'm afraid that I can't. I often lack the strength – You know that. You have seen me break down and cry, call out in agony and utter helplessness, begging for mercy from the pain in my heart and in my head.

I've been heavily hurt. You've watched me cry and beat myself up with guilt. Behind the girl with friends surrounding her is a lonely soul begging for a quiet moment. THIS is my quiet moment. THIS. Here.

Andrea wrote to me today. You seem to send me her letters just when I need them. It continues to amaze me when her feelings and experiences are a reflection of mine. We both seem to have hit a wall. It's like an accident that lasts nearly an entire week – about three days into the whole ordeal, I collapse. I think she is a part of me – a part that feels and breathes, cries and skips a beat, the part that often keeps me alive. Thank You.

I was thinking today about Hale-Bopp. I remember standing outside at night to watch the comet circling over our heads, pondering its existence. Among the stars of the evening sky is another natural phenomenon looking for a new place to live, a new place to shine. (When I say 'natural' phenomenon, I picture You chuckling to Yourself.)

I've been down on myself. Too tired to talk to anyone, too exhausted to share my feelings, my thoughts or my experiences. Lately the effort to know someone is too much for me. Is this selfish?

When I see a man put his arm around his wife and kiss her gently on the forehead, I feel myself becoming sad. They are truly one special couple in the midst of a thousand selfish people. I begin to recount the number of times I have been involved in a selfish love and, inside myself, I beg to be a part of something pure and unselfish.

I know there are other things to live for, God, but I want to be loved. I want to be protected and respected. I want to be held in the arms of someone who doesn't just understand me but who feels me. I want this person to swarm inside my veins, my flesh, my soul. I want him to pump my blood when my heart skips a beat. I want him to provide the cushion on which my heart sits, to promise not to whisk it away once my heart gets uncomfortable.

I want the universal language to be the heartbeat.

I have so many good things but something always seems to be misplaced. I think maybe the comet is asking me to come along – maybe I'll find what I'm looking for in the stars.

Your humble servant

I wrote 12 pages that night. I begged God for mercy, asked Him to be my wings, wondered if maybe He could give me some insight on how to become a better person. I knew I would never receive a direct answer but just knowing that I was completely honest was enough to tell that I hadn't done something useless.

From then on I wrote to God every night. My dark corner had a light shining upon it. When I needed a friend, someone to talk to, I turned to Him. It was nicer than having someone criticize or advise me and it's much better than asking a friend to ignore her life for a little while to tend to mine. God doesn't choose any one of us as more important or more worthy, which makes me sigh with relief.

Not much later I realized that everything I asked for in my letters to God were the things others prayed for. Suddenly praying no longer seemed forced or ritualistic – on the contrary, it came naturally and was easier than writing. I didn't have to come up with the words and it gave my hand a rest. All I had to do was open my Bahá'í prayer book and have some faith.

God, how does 10:00 tonight sound to you?

36

Prof Hamka Street

Aixa Maria Sobin

1917-born Mr Matni stood at a distance welcoming us. His face was as resplendent as the Padang sun which illuminated his gold-colored glasses. As we approached the wooden and tin shack which his friends had helped him to build, amidst the crowd and noise of the *oplets*, *bemos* and *citi ekpress'es*, he invited us in, although there was barely enough room in his shack for the three of us.

Pointing to all the small *klongtong* items surrounding us, he joyously said, 'This is my work, my bread and butter.' His bright eyes sunken beneath heavy eyelids, he sat down to give his crippled leg some rest. 'We must work, we must earn our life. We must get skills and expertise. We must produce fruits, people must benefit from us.' Fixing his faded multi-blue sarong with his 80-year-old wrinkled, tanned arm, he continued, 'God created us from the same stock, and made us higher than other creation. This can be an advantage or disadvantage, it depends on him or herself. A Persian Hidden Word says, 'Ye are the trees of My garden; ye must give forth goodly and wondrous fruits, that ye yourselves and others may profit therefrom.'[32]

Mr Matni used to earn a good living but since a neighbor set up another shop in front of his, he now earns around 3000 rupiah a day – a standard salary, according to other small shop owners in the area. For 1000 rupiah you can buy either half a kilo of sugar, half a kilo of oil or half a kilo of rice of the lowest grade. Three thousand is just small change. In order to grasp the value of 3000 rupiah, I decided to consult Dar, a cook at my friend's house who is known for thrift when bargaining for food at the local market. Dar thought that 3000 rupiah was not enough to enable two people to eat for one day.

In developing countries, many people earn a livelihood just to flee from poverty, not because they enjoy work, see work as worship of God or because they feel it is obligatory. Although Mr Matni's family does not have enough to live or eat well, this does not affect his outlook on life. Tidying his silver hair he added, '"It is incumbent on every one to engage in crafts and professions."[33] Work is worship.'

Some of the Bahá'ís in his area feel a responsibility towards him, as a member of their community, and want to support him financially. But Mr Matni does not want to accept it; he prefers to engage in a profession. Although his line of work does not keep him from living in poverty and he suffers from being physically challenged, he is happy. By working he feels he is fulfilling the purpose of his physical reality and is living according to the laws of the religion this Javanese man believes in, the Bahá'í Faith.

In the future, Mr Matni believes, every member of society will naturally help every other, thus putting an end to the ever-widening gap between wealth and poverty. If we are to eliminate this gap, the first prerequisite is the oneness of humankind. If we believe we all come from the same dust, we will care about the well-being of all, not just our own individual wealth. 'Wealth is most commendable, provided the entire population is wealthy,'[34] Mr Matni says, quoting 'Abdu'l-Bahá, for if we care for all equally, we cannot bear to see someone do without.

Mr Matni theorized, 'Perhaps in the future, there can be organizations set up to eliminate poverty. But as 'Abdu'l-Bahá said, it is impossible for everyone to be in the same [economic] position because everyone has different capacities, talents and intelligence. There should be no extremes but we cannot all be the same. Like an army. In an army everyone has a role but not everyone has the same role or position.'

As he smoothed over the crinkles in his sarong, this man from East Java continued, 'The peoples of the world are trying to eliminate poverty but failing. They cannot achieve it because they are prejudiced. With prejudice we cannot truly communicate. We are all interconnected but no one wants to be connected with us, with the poor.'

We need to acknowledge our ecological-like interdependence in order to achieve prosperity, as Mr Matni explains. 'If there is a seed, it will grow cooperatively with many elements; this is environmental unity. They work together in a united system and sacrifice here and there for the seed to grow and develop. Then when the seed turns into a tree and bears fruit, the fruit of the tree will be sacrificed for humanity to eat, to enjoy. And when humanity eats it, this unity becomes part of humanity. We must also sacrifice but this is based on our own will and we cannot force it. God has given man a choice, so it depends on our sacrifice or on the will of humanity.' Through his pearl-white smile Mr Matni continued, 'If we all have knowledge, then we will all support each other to have wealth.'

Days later, I learned that Mr Matni and his wife share their wealth. Some people are afraid to pass the shop because they will be given a for-sale item and they don't want Mr Matni's family to give away what little it has. But when the Matnis give away their things, they do it with such love that no one can refuse.

Friends know that Mr Matni's family gets great pleasure from giving to others and they don't want to take that pleasure away. So, in turn, many of his friends, because of the love they have for the family, give them some basic items they will need, just to help them a little.

As I walked away from Mr Matni's *toko* on Prof Hamka Street, I waved goodbye to the oldest Bahá'í in Indonesia: a man of true wealth.

37

Los Encinos

Amelia Villagómez

My parents were never 'save the earth' people but they always stressed the importance of being resourceful. My father is Mexican and was brought up in an area where people were rather poor – they just had less and dealt with it. My mother was born in Iran where nothing was ever wasted. She has told me stories about her life in Iran. When writing on paper for school, she had to write very lightly so she could go back, erase everything on it and reuse the paper. That concept is unheard of here in America, the land of plenty. In America, if we make a mistake, we wad up the paper and dunk it into the garbage. In Iran, food was never wasted. It was always either eaten entirely or saved for another meal.

When my mother came to America at 18 she was surprised by the habits of people living in this country. In Iran, since there was a short supply of nearly everything, people had to be very resourceful. In America, the shelves in grocery stores are stocked with paper and there are rows after rows of food, so we often forget to be resourceful. It took a trip to another country to teach me the lessons about materialism and conservation which my parents already knew.

One day my dad received a call inviting us to visit our relatives in Mexico. My parents decided this would be a good chance to see our relatives and to see how people in other parts of the world live. So my sister, my brother and I, along with our parents, journeyed south for an experience that proved to be very rewarding. Even though I was very young, this trip imprinted itself on my life very heavily.

The cheers that followed the announcement of our trip were soon transformed into tears. My siblings and I were expecting the glamorous, fancy trips you see on television – where you swim on the beaches all day and recline at a resort during the night. Our Mexico trip, however, was an entirely different matter.

Our family and my grandfather were crammed inside a pickup truck for three days and nights, without an air conditioner, in the sweltering heat of June. For what seemed like forever, we traveled with only each other.

'Ouch, get off my foot,' my sister complained.

'You're taking up too much space,' I whined back. We bickered back and forth to entertain ourselves. During the night, instead of staying at a hotel, we slept in our homey truck, with someone keeping guard, just in case. I remember that for the first part of the night, my parents kept guard and then my brother and sister would rotate on watch. I was exempt from this 'honor' because I was too young.

During our trip we crossed many mountains. With no paved roads, much of the ride was rocky. Many times we feared falling off the mountains because the roads were so narrow. There was only room for two cars to pass and when a large truck came our way, we would pray that we wouldn't be pushed off the mountain. The scenery was painted with only brown and blue paint. The desolate brown covered the mountains as far as we could see and the sky was painted a beautiful tranquil blue.

Finally, after many days of driving, we arrived at Los Encinos, high on a mountain with a population of about 200 people. No, Los Encinos is not a fancy resort but a village from which I trace my heritage. Materially it is poor but the people have a richness of the spirit and of the heart that is like a priceless pearl. The people who dwell in Los Encinos have spirits as high as the mountains themselves.

When we arrived, a group of children swarmed around our truck like bees in a hive. They were full of curiosity, wondering who we were and why we were there.

When you enter Los Encinos you take a step back a hundred years to a time when no one worried about crime and children sought comfort in each other instead of in drugs and alcohol. Beads of sweat were followed by tears of my heart at the sight my eyes beheld. After many days and nights on the road, we had finally arrived where I had originated – these were my roots. I met cousins I never knew I had and for the first time my spirit made a connection with the spirits of all those family members who had been born and lived in Mexico for hundreds of years. I wept.

LOS ENCINOS

Although Los Encinos wasn't a fancy resort, the people offered us the best they had. Mice filled our rooms but we slept on beds, unlike most of the people who lived in the area. We were very appreciative of the sacrifices they made for us to live in such comparable luxury. When we looked in the refrigerator, we saw tortillas, beans and five Cokes. They gave us each a Coke, which was like royal treatment, and they cooked with their best ingredients. The food was simple and it was wonderful because of the love and warmth with which it was made.

The shower was also an interesting experience. In America, a short shower may be 10 minutes long but in Los Encinos 10 minutes is a long time. The shower was prepared in a unique manner. There was a barrel on top of a small shower room. They lit a fire to heat the water. When the water was hot, we went in and took a quick shower under a slowly dripping shower head. We had to be quick so we wouldn't run out of water.

My relatives were poor in material goods but in other ways they were some of the wealthiest people on earth. Spiritually they dwelt on thrones. The little they had they offered to us, willingly and insistently giving with loving, open hands.

My most rewarding moment was handing out Jolly Ranchers. In America, Jolly Ranchers are just a little something you snack on during class when the teacher isn't watching but in Los Encinos it was a rare treat. My mother gave my brother and me two bags of Jolly Ranchers and encouraged us to distribute them to the other children as a small gift. As soon as the children saw the gold in our hands, they quickly formed a line around us. We then gave each child a Jolly Rancher, which brought smiles to their faces. How beautiful it was that these little things made them happy!

I've always wondered why some people are given so much and waste it, while others are given so much less, yet use it wisely. While staying at Los Encinos, I learned more of the unfairness in life than any book could illustrate. How could I waste food right and left when people of my own blood were content with tortillas, beans and chili? How could I whine for a new toy when my cousins were content just playing with each other? How could I whine about going to school, when I got to watch videos and learn how to use computers?

Mexico is not a poor country made up entirely of villages. There are large cities, stores, resorts, beaches and shopping malls. One summer my sister went to Monterrey. There she experienced a different and more materially luxurious way of life, yet noticed the same thread that runs throughout Mexico: the sweetness of the people – they are always giving and have pure hearts.

I began to question my standards. Although many people are materially richer than those of Los Encinos, the people of Los Encinos are wealthier in other ways. Material richness is a measure of tangible goods but real wealth is something different – it is something that comes from the heart. Material richness can be lost in a second but real wealth is carried on throughout life. If your goal is to become materially rich, you could wind up being poor in another sense. But if your aim to be wealthy in the spirit, you will be eternally happy. It doesn't make sense to have being rich as your goal in life because one day you will die and everything that you strived to earn will be lost. However, if you live from the standpoint of treating others kindly, living a pure life in which you respect and love everyone, then that virtue of goodness will be carried on with you as you progress in the other worlds of God.

When I crossed the border back to the United States, I brought higher values back into this country. In the process of advancing technologically, as a society we have diminished the importance of resourcefulness and being content. For example, we as a country waste a large amount of food, paper and electricity. Why? Because technology has allowed us to be so comfortable in our lives and has provided us the freedom and opportunity to care less about our resources – they seem so abundant. Children have learned, through television, that having a special toy will make them happier. As a society, we have been trained to want more. In contrast, in Mexico I learned values that remain with me, values which have been lost to many as technology has been gained, morals which must be retrieved for the progress of the soul and heart.

Although the trip to Los Encinos wasn't what I had anticipated, I greatly enjoyed it because of the immense love and warmth I felt. Los Encinos is a combination of great poverty and great wealth and from it I learned of the great imbalance of life. We can't continue being a world of opposites. We must unite and help our brothers and sisters. We must learn from each other and share each other's wealth. Then we will be both materially comfortable and spiritually wealthy.

38

A Moment

Holley Seals

Sitting in a constricting airplane seat for 14 hours, with only so many comfort options, can be somewhat unpleasant. However, I would never say that the trouble I endure getting to where I am going isn't worth it in the end. This is the price of traveling – something I am madly in love with.

This love has taken me from my home in the southern United States to Canada, Central America, Europe and, most recently, to the Arab Emirates where I had a three-day layover while en route to a land I once only dreamt of. I am most definitely a world citizen and this land I am referring to was my latest adventure. It cast a new light on my perception of the world and its many inhabitants. I went to Africa.

First, let me say that one of my earliest wishes from childhood was to see a real African sunset. I don't know if it was the magnificence of size or the brilliance of colors that swarmed in my young imagination, enrapturing me. But I am positive it was written somewhere in my destiny to step into that faraway place – to see it through my own eyes rather than the eyes of *National Geographic*. To feel the warmth grace my skin, to 'know' it, rather than just imagine it.

And so through unexpected circumstances, as things fell into place rather mystically, following my graduation from high school I left my secure home on lucky St Patrick's day and began my Bahá'í year of service. I ventured to the unknown glory that awaited me on the other side of the world.

My welcome was perfection. We had left Abu Dhabi hours before and I was recording my every emotion and thought in my constant companion – my journal – when the captain's slightly muffled voice broke through the still cabin, saying, 'We have just come to the coastal shore of the Motherland. Relatively speaking, it won't be too much farther now.'

Curious, I lifted my window shade and with squinting eyes peered out to witness the most dazzling rainbow of pinks, oranges and reds that I had ever seen combined. There was a seraphic flood of firelight drowning the sky – seraphic because it was at that moment that I realized the glorious power surrounding me. There were streaks of fluorescent flames stretched across the highlighted clouds and cradled in this ocean of brilliance balanced a red-honeyed sphere of complex perfection. The sun's flawless shape, its overpowering size, its resilient timelessness: my eyes were glued.

And finally, I could replace in my mind the media's two-dimensional paper image of the sunset with my own vision of grandeur. My eyes were granted their long-ago wish of an African sunset and my feet were yet to touch the ground. All the while, I was insufficiently trying to relay the overwhelming feelings from my body to the lined paper that lay before me. And so I watched the African sun retreat into its temporary shelter until the following morning, when it would again visibly rule the earth. For some reason, I didn't think twice about the fact that the sun looked to be setting right into the horizon of the land, although I knew that the ground lay thousands of feet below me. I watched with brimming tears as it sank into its cover and my heart graciously thanked whatever essence allowed me to be where I was at that moment.

With all the beauty the sky exhibited, those of us who happened to be looking out our tiny windows were given a second gift. The present was unwrapped ever so slowly and I watched in awe as the darkened clouds – the horizon I had mistaken for land – slowly parted, melting into the rest of the sky. And there was the crimson fireball floating in its perfect space. Never would my mind have conjured up such a sight. I did not know that such a routine event as the sun setting could contain so much power and evoke the same power within me. It was exquisite.

To this day, I couldn't tell you all that it did to me to witness a 'double' sunset in the land that had held my dreams for so long but now, inside, I am different. I can say that I search for life's minute moments of purity and beauty in everything I see. I search for those moments that pass unnoticed in the daily rush of life. But somehow, in the calm of their silence, lies the inspiration craved by every living being, the kind that poets dream of, that artists live to capture, that prayerful souls seek. Now, I take time to stare at life until I find whatever it was that has drawn my eyes. I listen closely to the words that people don't say between the words they do. I pay homage to silence, to stillness, to space. I honor the times that reveal the intricate truths of life. They are everywhere and not always hidden, I know.

I am forever searching for that jewel that only appreciative eyes can see – that moment of unexpected glory comparable to the beauty I once found through a tiny airplane window. The moment that was simply the beginning.

Bibliography

'Abdu'l-Bahá. *Paris Talks*. London: Bahá'í Publishing Trust, 1995.

— *The Promulgation of Universal Peace.*
Wilmette, IL: Bahá'í Publishing Trust, 1982.

— *The Secret of Divine Civilization.*
Wilmette, IL: Bahá'í Publishing Trust, 1990.

— *Selections from the Writings of 'Abdu'l-Bahá.*
Haifa: Bahá'í World Centre, 1978.

— *Some Answered Questions.*
Wilmette, IL: Bahá'í Publishing Trust, 1981.

Bahá'í Prayers: A Selection of Prayers revealed by Bahá'u'lláh, the Báb and 'Abdu'l-Bahá. Wilmette, IL: Bahá'í Publishing Trust, 1991.

Bahá'u'lláh. *Gleanings from the Writings of Bahá'u'lláh.*
Wilmette, IL: Bahá'í Publishing Trust, 1983.

— *The Hidden Words.*
Wilmette, IL: Bahá'í Publishing Trust, 1990.

— *The Kitáb-i-Aqdas.*
Haifa: Bahá'í World Centre, 1992.

— *Tablets of Bahá'u'lláh.*
Wilmette, IL: Bahá'í Publishing Trust, 1988.

Compilation of Compilations, The. Prepared by the Universal House of Justice 1963-1990. 2 vols.
Sydney: Bahá'í Publications Australia, 1991.

Lights of Guidance: A Bahá'í Reference File. Compiled by Helen Hornby. New Delhi: Bahá'í Publishing Trust, 2nd edn. 1988.

Women: A Compilation of Extracts from the Bahá'í Writings.
London: Bahá'í Publishing Trust, rev. edn. 1990.

References

1. 'Abdu'l-Bahá, *Selections*, p. 302.

2. Bahá'u'lláh, *Hidden Words*, Arabic no. 5.

3. Bahá'u'lláh, *Gleanings*, p. 336.

4. 'Abdu'l-Bahá, *Promulgation*, p. 453.

5. 'Abdu'l-Bahá, *Selections*, p. 205.

6. 'Abdu'l-Bahá, *Paris Talks*, p. 98.

7. 'Abdu'l-Bahá, *Promulgation*, pp. 427–8.

8. Bahá'u'lláh, *Gleanings*, p. 250.

9. 'Abdu'l-Bahá, in *Women*, p. 11.

10. Bahá'u'lláh, Fire Tablet, in *Bahá'í Prayers*, p. 220.

11. Bahá'u'lláh, *Gleanings*, pp. 184–5.

12. ibid. p. 177.

13. ibid.

14. ibid.

15. ibid.

16. Bahá'u'lláh, *Hidden Words*, Persian no. 5.

17. 'Abdu'l-Bahá, *Some Answered Questions*, pp. 22–8.

18. Bahá'u'lláh, *Gleanings*, p. 250.

19. 'Abdu'l-Bahá, *Paris Talks*, p. 189.

20. From a letter written by Shoghi Effendi to an individual believer, 8 December 1935, in *Lights of Guidance*, p. 543.

21. Bahá'u'lláh, *Kitáb-i-Aqdas*, para. 149.

22. From a letter written on behalf of Shoghi Effendi to an individual believer, 26 February 1933, in *Lights of Guidance*, p. 625.

23. 'Abdu'l-Bahá, quoted in *Compilation*, vol. 1, p. 397.

24. 'Abdu'l-Bahá, *Paris Talks*, pp. 95–6.

25. Bahá'u'lláh, *Kitáb-i-Aqdas*, para. 31.

26. ibid. para. 115.

27. 'Abdu'l-Bahá, *Promulgation*, p. 175.

28. ibid. p. 300.

29. ibid. p. 317.

30. Bahá'u'lláh, *Tablets*, pp. 51–2.

31. Bahá'u'lláh, *Kitáb-i-Aqdas*, para. 51.

32. Bahá'u'lláh, *Hidden Words*, Persian no. 80.

33. ibid.

34. 'Abdu'l-Bahá, *Secret of Divine Civilization*, p. 24.